RESPONSIBILITY

AND

PUBLIC SERVICES

Richard Davis

Foreword by John Seddon

Published by:
Triarchy Press
Station Offices
Axminster
Devon
EX13 5PF
United Kingdom
+44 (0)1297 631456

info@triarchypress.net
www.triarchypress.net

A catalogue record for this book is available from the British Library.

Print ISBN: 978–1–909470–83–5

Contents

Foreword   v

PART ONE

Introduction   1

Chapter 1   9
Design against demand (the contextual needs of the citizen)

Chapter 2   21
Pull not push

Chapter 3   35
Expertise not Services

Chapter 4   39
Using data

Chapter 5   53
Principles and practices for making change happen

Chapter 6   61
Leadership

Chapter 7   71
The Economic case

PART TWO   82
The Logic of the Current System

Chapter 8   83
Getting things done in the current system

Chapter 9   95
Getting value for money

Chapter 10   107
Keep us safe

Chapter 11   111
The citizen's relationship with the state

Part Two Summary   116

Conclusion   118

A call to arms   118

About the Author
About the Publisher

Foreword

Whichever way you look at it, public services provided for people whose lives have fallen off the rails consume a very large proportion of expenditure. The Whitehall narrative has it that there is an immediate and growing crisis: demand is rising, so who will pay?

Richard Davis shows through an evidence-based narrative that the crisis – if we should call it that – is a crisis of management, organisation and political policy. In short, we waste hundreds of millions of pounds on ineffective and counter-productive interventions.

The opportunity to radically lower the costs of services is nothing short of breath-taking, to say nothing of the beneficial consequences for people's lives and the quality of life in communities.

Richard Davis, one of the founding members of Vanguard, is respected by his colleagues and clients for his profundity of insight and practical competence. He has pioneered Vanguard's work in this field. As early adopters of the ideas in this book have found, the ideas may challenge conventional wisdom but they are logical, practical and effective.

Anybody involved in services will gain enormous value from the guidance Richard provides. Policy makers, if they take the time to first understand what is described here, will realise that policy should be concerned with the State getting out of the way of people who, if given responsibility, can seize the opportunity to improve services.

In turn, better services will have a profound impact on the level of expenditure. What could be more important?

John Seddon

PART ONE

Introduction

A social services manager discovered for herself how well the system was working for the people it was designed to care for. Her reaction was profound: "I felt physically sick. I went home and decided that all I could do was to resign – I was responsible for this awful failure." She was not responsible, but her discovery raised an important question: Why have we designed public services in such a way that they fail to deliver what matters? The cost of failure is huge and a waste of public money but, worse, and as the manager discovered, services can sometimes do more harm than good.

I have written this book for those of you who work in the public sector who would like to find real solutions to people's needs. There is little point in trying to explain how to do this to politicians or public sector leaders. The politicians want simple answers delivered quickly and seem unable to understand why there is a need to rethink the logic and redesign public services; and it is my contention that public sector leaders, influenced by Blair's ruthless pressure to deliver on targets, have developed a Whitehall mentality where the purpose is simply to 'make the numbers'.

It is very difficult to find any useful leadership in the public sector – those who might provide focus and inspiration are looking at their performance numbers and not at the public they serve. However, I believe that this is actually good news on another level. It leaves the way open for operational managers and locally elected politicians to become leaders, to take control and make a difference. This is precisely what is happening in the public sector areas that we, Vanguard, are involved in. Historically it was unheard of for the elected members to be part of the work but now they are willing and influential partners giving much needed backing, understanding and enthusiasm to the operational managers.

As it is, the public sector doesn't function very well. This is a statement that can be verified from many viewpoints – complaints about the National Health Service (NHS) and police services continue to rise, education standards have stalled, access to social services is ever more difficult and local authorities are struggling to provide what people see as basic services, such as libraries and pothole repairs. My own work in the public sector has shown it to be inefficient and largely ineffective – it's simply not good at delivering what matters. It is awash with money and yet all that is heard is the clamour for more. We tend to believe the media narrative that the quality of services is directly related to funding and nothing else. We have created a narrative of doom about costs: 'We are living longer, families are broken, treatments are more expensive, the health and care bill will be out of control... '. This is plausible but a *non sequitur*. There is no evidential link between an ageing population and a much higher need for services, yet it is 'true' in most people's minds. A recent report in the *BMJ*[1], for example, clarified that the increase in demand on the NHS was largely down to medical practice – over-diagnosis, unnecessary procedures, fragmented and uncoordinated treatment and the unnecessary use of expensive technology. Data show that the elderly add only about 2% to NHS costs[2]. A study in Canada also concluded that the impending 'catastrophe' of the ageing populations is a myth[3].

So why are we in this mess with poorly performing services? As citizens, as humans, we like to attribute success and failure to a group of individuals. It helps us to explain things to ourselves and each other with a 'convincing' narrative. The blame usually falls on a predictable set of suspects – the unions, Westminster politicians, the civil service, and the belief that the workforce in frontline public sector organisations are inefficient and badly managed. Vanguard's experience, however, is that there is nothing wrong with any particular group of people but that there is much wrong with the system within which they work and of which they have to try and make some sense. Nonetheless, it's very difficult to accept an argument that says 'it's not the people who are at fault, it's the system that's at fault'.

Politicians are responsible for the design and running of the system. They are responsible for making decisions based on knowledge. They are responsible for understanding the connection between the design, the way the public sector works and how the workers behave. And we need to ask those politicians some serious questions about the design when people start blaming the police for being dishonest about their crime statistics!

Every government comes to power promising a better set of policies and practices. It usually rails against the previous government's incompetence and then, somewhere along the line, it decides that it was alright really, that they just didn't do the work properly. Governments are the masters of Ackoff's[4] proposition, that most of our problems arise from

1 *British Medical Journal.* BMJ 2014;349:g4818.
2 www.cms.gov/Research–Statistics–Data–and–Systems/Statistics–Trends–and–Reports/Nation-alHealthExpendData/downloads/tech_2000_0810.pdf
3 Barer, M.L., Hertzman,C. 'Apocalypse No: population aging and the future of health care system', SEDAP Research Paper No. 59
4 *Financial Times*, 9 November 2009. 'Fond farewell to a brilliant thinker', Byline: Stefan Stern. – See www.ft.com/cms/s/0/0168c7de–cd7e–11de–8162–00144feabdc0.html#axzz3iayD9uHk

doing the wrong thing righter. The public sector workforce and the citizen are told that each new government policy is going to make things better, and yet both end up with different versions of the same ineffectiveness.

Is there an alternative to the current system? And if there is, how would we know if it was any better? Some parts of the system will always be political – based on the values that politicians wish to promote. However, most changes should be based on empirical evidence (what works). Current political thinking takes little notice of this. For example, there is a growing body of empirical evidence that shows that children learn better if academic learning is delayed and early learning is focused on socialisation, but UK government policy is instead bolstering academic content in the early years. Recent governments have made great play of evidence-based policies yet regularly ignore the contribution of the experts they consult and employ.

One wonders on what basis and with what evidence politicians do design their systems! It purports to be common sense and thus to carry some apparent authority, but many decisions are based on nothing more than plausibility – we just kid ourselves that it is common sense. This is why empiricism, finding out what actually works, is so vital.

Let's look at Margaret Thatcher's policy to bring the public sector into the realms of professional business practice. The argument was, indeed, plausible; if the public purse is paying for these organisations, the public should expect nothing less than full accountability and assurance that their money is well spent. There were three assumptions:

1. the private sector is efficient
2. the private sector model can be transferred to the public sector
3. the public sector is inefficient.

Assumption 1 – the private sector is efficient

One example of the private sector failing to produce efficiency is in the motor insurance trade. Insurers have commissioned third parties to manage various parts of the claims process in order to harvest the kickbacks. These third parties are paid on the financial value of the job and so readily inflate it, and insurance premiums have to rise to accommodate the practice. In practice, the market behaves like a monopoly.

Decades of experience with private sector companies has shown that they all operate on the same business philosophy – they have the same set of assumptions about what a 'good' organisation looks like and how it is run. They all build the same waste and failure into their systems and practices. The result is that the good ones are merely the best of a bad set.

Assumption 2 – the private sector model can be transferred to the public sector

Can the private sector model ever be applied to the public sector? The answer is 'yes', but not the model currently being used which is based on Adam Smith's notion of division of labour and economies of scale. Smith had a clear goal – to make products as cheap as possible and as many of them as possible in order to allow the British mercantile system to dominate the world market. It was all about cost efficiency and supply – the more you make the more you sell. Organisations in developed countries have followed the logic, and it is now so ingrained that most people have forgotten its roots and don't ask themselves if this method will solve the problems they are facing today.

Similarly, managerial methods were established a long time ago. In the late 1800s there was a serious rail accident (rail companies were all private companies at the time) in New England. An enquiry was convened to find out who was at fault. In the process, specific responsibilities were established for the company's hierarchy to ensure that it was absolutely clear who would be accountable for any failure in future. The incident is widely believed to have been responsible for the establishment of the hierarchy as an accountability system and not simply as a means of ensuring productive capacity. Combined with Smith's logic, the basis of the management system as we know it today was established, ensuring both outputs and accountability. The elements of what has been called the second industrial revolution – oil prospecting, extraction, refinement and distribution, coupled with assembly line production systems – simply reinforced the need for such management.

The separation of operation from management, which comes from the natural hierarchy of supervision accountability, has created characteristic managerial behaviour. This varies depending on the assumptions about what makes a good manager (administrative, financial or technical, for example). What does not appear to vary very much is how senior managers become absorbed into the 'management factory' and rely on the hierarchy for communication. This has added the feature of top-down management which can be described as 'command and control'.

The logic and practice of command and control dramatically alters the nature of 'knowledge'. Knowledge is not just cast in terms of cost efficiency as a measure of success but it is determined by the characteristics of the up and down flow of the hierarchy. It is never, therefore, direct knowledge but only ever second-hand at best. Some may point to IT systems as giving a form of direct access, but then who designed the IT system and for what purpose. The answer is usually, 'it was designed for the management, in order to keep the management factory going.'

The system learns to convince itself that it has knowledge. We need to be critical of this so-called knowledge and assess it for what it is and is not. Recent governments have been tackling the problem of how to get people off benefits and back to work. They claim to have knowledge of how to achieve this, but Andrew Mawson[5], one of the UK's leading social entrepreneurs, questions this. In his book, *The Social Entrepreneur*, he shows how to achieve exactly what government is striving for. He shows the need to pay attention to what matters to people in the local community, engage them in rebuilding it and, through that, build skills and confidence that allows and encourages them to thrive and develop. He details the formidable struggle he has had to convince ministers and the civil servants that this model is worth supporting. It is clear that if it doesn't fit government policy it doesn't happen. Knowledge of what works takes a back seat. He had much success in getting ministers' interest but great difficulty getting that interest translated into cogent and substantive support, despite the fact that his work has decades of evidence.

It is a moot point as to whether ministers can be held accountable for this failure to understand how to use evidence to build policy and create effective methods of implementation. They could have learned from Toyota, but then very few others did. Toyota introduced a fundamentally different set of assumptions about the design of organisations, but most leaders in the west, both political and industrial, missed the logic[6]. They could have sought more evidence and knowledge but the 'big four' accountancy and consultancy companies, on whom they all rely for such knowledge, also missed the logic.

I started this section by saying that private sector models can be applied to the public sector but that it depends on the thinking behind the model. What characterises the Toyota revolution is that the system is designed backwards. The emphasis is not on production efficiency but on meeting consumer demand. If a customer orders a particular model then the system starts with that order and works backwards to plan what will be required to make that car. Toyota calls this a 'pull system' – each step determines what is 'pulled' from the line to complete the car[7]. If the operating model in both sectors were to change to a Toyota style pull system, where the nature of demand determines the design of the system, then the answer to the question of whether the private and public sectors are comparable is, yes. Taiichi Ohno, the Chief Engineer of Toyota and its revolution, said that he had looked at mass production (in the 1950s) and

---

5 Mawson, A. (2008) *The Social Entrepreneur*. Atlantic Books
6 Toyota is now in trouble but recent poor decisions should not take away from the logic that made it successful.
7 Other manufacturers would claim to have followed this logic, but while they may change their processes, few would seem to have understood the philosophy.

could not see a market for which it was suited. While Adam Smith saw that economy of scale was the foundation for cost reduction, Ohno saw economy of flow as the basis of success; in other words, design the right flow for each demand and costs will be reduced. Smith's system was based on the economy being driven by supply (the more you make the more you sell) whereas Ohno's was based on demand – understand what people want to buy, make sure that you can make it and then make to order.

At a stroke Ohno not only challenged the basic idea that underpins current public and private sector management but he showed that cost reduction is successful and sustainable when it is a consequence of designing good work – without waste. In other words, trying to manage a process in order to create cost reduction is a fool's errand. His ideas have succeeded in Japan for 60 years but we can't see it for looking. If it is any consolation, much of Japanese business has not seen it either.

Assumption 3 – the public sector is inefficient

As I have said before, there is a consensus that the public sector is badly managed, with repeated reports in the media condemning the services' failure to protect our most vulnerable citizens and/or to avoid the squandering of taxpayers' money. The discrepancy between what matters to us and what matters to politicians is, in itself, a major barrier to effective running of the public sector. To ordinary people, the public sector is the set of organisations they deal with: health, education, police, local authorities and the specialist agencies, such as the Driver and Vehicle Licensing Agency (DVLA). However, to the politician the public sector is two entities: the organisations the public deal with and the civil service through which their knowledge of and access to the frontline organisations is interpreted and put into action.

I can only guess that the politicians' view of the public sector is coloured by their relationship with the civil service but there seems to be a cherished belief that public servants have a 'jobsworth' tendency, are divorced from the real world and wouldn't recognise the notion of efficiency if they fell over it in the street – 'They need reforming', 'They are fat and bloated'. The question is, on what evidence and from what perspective can they make these judgements? As noted before, given the inefficiency of the private sector, any comparison is invidious.

Mass production logic has infected government and the public sector. The logic has become an obsession for politicians. They must be seen to be managing an efficient system. Blair's 'deliverology' highlighted the fact that politicians have actually become managers. They micro-manage the country and specify the way work is done.

The public sector, in government eyes, should be accountable. It should exploit economy of scale for cost efficiencies and citizens should have the advantages of being treated as customers. Does that not sound utterly plausible? Who would/could argue with those propositions? Is there a better definition of motherhood and apple pie?

It is my contention that it is these three assumptions that have seriously undermined the public sector and filled it with waste and inefficiency. This is not a political argument. In the following chapters I shall take these notions one at a time and test the arguments.

The blame for this waste and inefficiency should actually be ascribed to a toxic combination of ideological beliefs (political, economic and managerial) that prevent policy-makers from being able to see the all-pervasive broken models of conventional management at work in the sector. The systemic blindness to the broken delivery chain is such that politicians remain caught in a self-reinforcing loop, where their prescriptions for change only ever result in a larger dose of 'more of the same' to their ailing public-sector patient.

I will argue that improvement requires a degree of political determination to escape this cycle, and a simultaneous, renewed commitment to empiricism: a better understanding of 'what works'. By following this path of empiricism, politicians can start to think about new models of service delivery. The main purpose of the book, however, is to encourage managers, and indeed anyone else in the public sector, to follow the example of those of their colleagues who are already using a different way of thinking to make a real difference and to achieve much better results.

The first part of the book describes the new set of principles which are in operation, what that means for citizens and how you can make them work for your own systems. The second part of the book shows how current thinking undermines the new logic. The government approach appears sensible in that it demands results, efficiency, safety and choice. It is important, therefore, to know the arguments and how to accommodate and counter them. It also seeks to give guidance on what managers will need in order to make successful change happen.

In spite of the obvious success you will read about, the work described can sometimes be seen as a 'warm and fluffy' option rather than a mainstream alternative. But what we need to find out is how well it meets the three goals of getting things done, spending money wisely and protecting citizens –we know that the new model is cheaper and more effective but we need more weight of evidence to present to policy makers. I review the economics of a new system and provide guidance on change and leadership.

Chapter 1

Design against demand
(the contextual needs of the citizen)

The current system understands demand as a transaction, e.g. a phone call. It sets handling standards (answer within x seconds) and target measures (y% of calls to be answered) against that transaction and seeks to reduce the cost at all times. From the perspective of the citizen, services designed around these 'transactions' rarely supply what they need and are just a wasteful part of the process.

We carried out some research for Advice UK on how well the voluntary advice sector was working. Advice organisations, local and national, help people struggling with decisions around the granting of disability allowances. They manage cases and provide advocacy. Of all the cases going to tribunal, 93% were found in favour of the plaintiff. This is eyebrow-raising in itself but the real learning comes when you find out that the agencies involved (as they were then) rarely got their sums wrong. The decisions were technically accurate but the judges found that the context had been ignored. In other words, the person had been ignored. So, for example, a person with mental health problems was deemed by the Department for Work and Pensions (DWP) to have 'recovered' and the support was withdrawn. The reality, as noted in the tribunal decision, was that it was precisely that support that enabled the person to cope. When it was withdrawn the recovery was reversed. The point is that the transactions – the technical aspects – don't take 'context' into account. For the citizen, context means, 'Do you understand me and my life?'

People from every agency we work with talk about and *believe* that they deal in 'person-centred' services. So to conclude that we need to change the public sector from a transactional perspective to a person-centred perspective will simply get the eyes rolling. The problem for most people is trying to fathom why anyone would design a system that was not person-centred. But design it they did. It is equally difficult for practitioners – how could they admit to themselves that they are not person-centred?

A better focus might be one that tackles effectiveness and efficiency, the goal being to do exactly what matters at first point of contact – either the issue is resolved for the citizen, or the right processes are designed so that problems can be resolved as efficiently as possible for all concerned. This is the critical concept that initiates change. It is the place for leaders to begin to understand what the process *could* look like, and then (when you've tried it) what it *does* look like. The new way of thinking, doing only what matters, becomes much clearer both in principle and in practice. The paradoxical aspect is that when you seek to improve effectiveness in this way, the efficiency improves all on its own.

A Case Study
Stoke City Council

The leaders of the functional departments at Stoke City Council had been learning what worked for citizens and what did not. They had also involved other agencies, such as Fire & Rescue and the police services. They took the decision to set up a multi-agency team that would be capable, as they saw it, of best handling a range of issues.

The first problem was how to identify people who needed help. One view was that any of the contact points in the council would suffice because people would bring something somewhere and the real problems could be picked up after contact. The other view was to understand what happens in a given geographical area – unknowns included the relationship between a geographical area and its people as well as the relationships between the people themselves. Given that a goal is to build strength in the community itself, this seemed to the Stoke team to be the obvious way forward. They worked with the local politicians and chose a ward that was representative without being extreme. The next step was to find out what issues the people had and what mattered to people in that ward.

It is easy to over-plan this activity. The truth is that people will only talk to your agency about things that they believe you will act on. Therefore, the probability is that you will never know what the issues are until you engage with them anyway. Start somewhere and learn how to find people. The Stoke team soon found that visiting the housing department and connecting with housing officers was a very quick way to find people who needed help.

The next problem was how to get people's trust. Why would people trust agencies that have seldom provided any effective help? But this became straightforward. The task was to understand demand (in context) from the citizen's perspective, which involved asking a set of simple questions. They discovered that it was just these two questions that seemed to work:

- What does a good life look like?
- What works /does not work for you in your life at the moment?

The team found this a deceptively simple concept – it is so obvious. Yet in practice, they found careful listening, summarising and demonstrating that they had understood what they had been told, a difficult skill. People are not used to being listened to.

The conversations were recorded verbatim and then the key phrases extracted. It is too easy to fit what is said into preconceived notions of what matters so this is an important step.

For the team's benefit, the recurring themes were then collated, and five stood out.

- Help me get/keep a job.
- Help me manage my finances/claim benefit.
- Help me move to a more suitable property.
- Help me live closer to friends and family.
- Help me keep my home.

This is not a generic demand analysis and it is certainly not a blueprint for service design but it does indicate the skills that the team were likely to need to pull on. Although there will be similar needs expressed elsewhere (people are people) this must be treated as the picture for just this ward in Stoke.

The next thing of interest is to work out how representative the data is and what patterns it shows across the ward. Plotting the data from various agencies on a map, a significant overlap was found[1]. A relatively small number of properties/families were involved at this stage and all were in social housing developments. This was then a working map to which other families/properties could be added as they emerged.

Many people planning this type of research ask us how we know if we have identified all the demand. We don't; but what Stoke found was that as citizens realise that you can be trusted and that what you do works for them, they talk to each other and word of mouth finds the others ("You helped me, can you help her?", "You did this for my neighbour, can you do it for me?")[2].

The Stoke team now had a reasonable picture of demand by geography. They knew not to generalise – each ward would need its own analysis. They had an understanding of what mattered to people, what problems they needed to solve in context and the extent of these problems. The next step was to design against that demand. The risk at this point was for the team to fall back into designing solutions for each of these top five categories. This would miss the point. Solutions will emerge for each

---

1 The only issue not to correlate was child protection.
2 People will only speak to you about things they think you will act on. It is an iterative process – the more you do well, the more they will tell you.

person as team members gain knowledge and engage the individuals in what will work for them. The design process is a learning process:

- How do we learn what works?
- What is the connection and interdependence between the apparent problems?
- What does the outcome of solving a problem look like?
- How do we build resilience in the person, family and network?

Design became simply a process of 'pick a person who needs help, get the best resource to take responsibility for providing that help and see what we can learn'. This is still work in progress.

The first challenge was to decide how to begin with each person. The most important early outcome was to build trust and demonstrate a different relationship between citizen and services. Then help was provided based on something that mattered to the person.

Some examples

A woman suffered from agoraphobia. The team arranged for her to have a garden bench so that she could begin the process of feeling comfortable outside.

A family moved into a new property and found waste items had been left behind by the previous tenant. Multiple requests to remove them had not been actioned. Getting them removed proved to be enough to make them feel that the team genuinely wanted to help.

A woman suffered from alopecia and had become a recluse as a consequence. The team bought her a wig.

A tenant was on the verge of being evicted for failing to keep his property maintained. The team arranged for him to have a lawn mower, which he was very happy about, and this started the process of turning the relationship with the housing department around.

Another woman was struggling to feed her family. She didn't have a cooker and was relying on bought meals. The team arranged for her to have a cooker.

These all seem trivial issues but they were very important to the citizens in question. They heralded the new approach and a new relationship – someone really did want to help.

~~~

This learning-from-design method can be fitted into a framework. There are three levels of support to be considered and, therefore, three different sets of problems to solve.

Think of it as a pyramid (Diagram 1). At the base is most of the population who need little in the way of intervention and who feel their lives are under their own control. The middle section are those who are struggling, either temporarily because of unforeseen events, or permanently due to not being able to control themselves or their context. At the top of the pyramid is a small section of the population who experience or create serious problems.

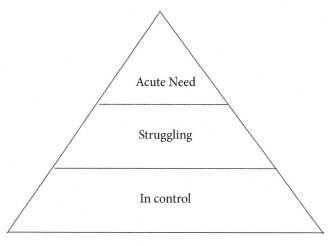

Diagram 1

The base of the pyramid – those in control of their own lives – is where most of us operate from. What do we need? Very little, in practice. We need good quality information so that we can make informed choices. We are not a 'market', we simply know what we want; for example we want services to work when we use them. With good information we can usually be self–regulating and our choices will determine the organisations we use. As far as public sector organisations are concerned (with the exception of education and health) they will be notable by their absence. For people in this category, the agencies simply need to focus on creating information and making it available. Agencies are indeed putting a lot of information on websites and where this is done to provide what matters to citizens as opposed to internal attempts to reduce staff, then it is an important contribution. The test will be how well the content is monitored against demand.

Useful information about performance data from the user's perspective – i.e. how well does the service really solve users' problems – would be helpful. A good example of a model for this sort of 'user' information is JD Power *(www.jdpower.com)* based in the USA. It provides collated data about aspects of owning cars that matter to the owners. Another, in the UK, is the Doctor Foster site (*drfoster.com*) which provides data to healthcare professionals and the public about the track record of medical services and procedures.

The middle of the pyramid. This group is made up of people from a very disparate set of circumstances, from people guilty of an unwitting or 'out of character' infringement (a speeding fine, for example) to someone with a so-called chaotic lifestyle (the effects of drugs, alcohol, unemployment). For those who have ended up with the latter problems, the 'professionals' take charge, and label and process them – completely out of context. They will see only the symptoms: an alcohol problem, rather than the underlying person who is struggling.

Many professionals will know the consequence of failing to intervene early and will understand that costs go up over time. But what they do not see is that the way they currently intervene not only fails to help, but in many cases actively increases the instability. The actual cost of current interventions would surprise them.

The failure of the existing system pushes people into the top of the pyramid. While there are obvious examples, such as a failure to rehabilitate offenders, and indeed the failure to identify damaged children early on in their lives, the problem is far more common than we think.

This is the group that the Stoke initiative is focusing on and, as above, the skills and learning will be used to strengthen the context and resolve problems.

The top of the pyramid – those in crisis. The public sector will never be without services in a traditional sense and, for those in crisis, these services traditionally work well. In emergencies or when problems are critical, the police and the local authorities do an excellent job. However, when people who are just struggling are not helped they can easily reach crisis point. Unfortunately, it is these people who create 'noise' in the system (viz A&E), which still fails to help them, and which obscures the needs of those in real crisis.

The following are two examples of 'noise' that diminish the capacity of the system to see where the real problems lie.

1) There is a high demand for speech and language therapists in the education field. Parents are understandably concerned when their children struggle to read and/or write and want dedicated support for them. This can create pressure to label children because the label attracts funding. But how many of those children are actually dyslexic or have listening, reading or writing difficulties? How many are simply struggling because their parents sit them in front of a TV and don't talk to them very much? How often does it need a therapist and how often does it simply need someone to understand the child in context? We don't have the data because we don't see it that way. Inevitably, though, there will be far more children being 'treated' than is necessary and genuinely needy children will be buried in the 'noise'. I was struck by a mother talking on the radio a few years back whose child was trilingual at the age of seven when she entered the English system. The mother remarked sardonically, 'Isn't it funny that my daughter is only dyslexic in English?'

2) An ambulance driver told me that he has to respond three times a week to a lady who has become addicted to oxygen after she found she could get ambulance crews to supply it. She was just one of the many cases he could describe. Across the spectrum, these people are creating demand which falls between the cracks of the agencies and is deemed too expensive to resolve.

The proposition that I believe needs to be tested is whether we can support people and help them to support themselves so that they will be pulled back into the stable base of the triangle. And will that in turn improve their lives whilst reducing cost in the system? Here are two examples of this in action.

1) Gloucester social care teams identified a group of 19 people who had been earmarked for residential care (a last resort that is normally irrevocable). But, after finding out what mattered to them and acting on it, all 19 people were able to live (happily and confidently) in their own homes. In one case, for example, this was simply the need for a wheelchair so that the person could get around the house. The system had previously refused to supply it as she was not deemed eligible. In another case, social care provided help for the family. With the cost of residential care at, on average, £800 per person per week, supporting people in their own home is a simple and effective saving. And what did it mean for those 19 people to stay comfortably and without worry in their own homes and close to friends, family and neighbours?

2) The dementia care team in Raglan worked hard to rebuild people's connections in the community. These people had been previously 'written off' as beyond support and unresponsive. The results were astonishing. Not only were these patients able to have a very good quality of life but not one of them, so far, has been admitted to hospital, something that would have been constant and normal in the previous system. What's more the team's workload actually went down.

Looking at the care of people who are in hospital

The re-design team was looking at the discharge regime, but also wanted to look at the complete end-to-end experience for the patient and the hospital. A ward nurse identified a patient as being typical of the patients she had to deal with and, therefore, typically problematic. Her parting shot was to wish the team "good luck – he's very uncooperative, aggressive and we can't do anything with him". (Time and again, the most compelling stories are about people who would normally have been written off by the system.) The team found out quickly that he was virtually blind, a fact that had not been picked up by the hospital staff. He was a little autistic and had an extreme fear of authority and institutions. His overwhelming concern was the guide dog that he'd had to leave at home. Healthcare professionals made untested assumptions about his home circumstances and decided that he needed to be admitted for his own safety. If his problems had been understood at all, he could have been supported in a very different way. The team managed to settle him down by simply talking about what mattered to him, and then worked on how to get him out of hospital and back with his dog.

Here are some examples in more detail to show how understanding people in context can work:

Marjorie is 73 and has been living with cancer for 12 years. Her husband died some years ago. She has no children and lives alone, although she has a good network of friends and neighbours in her local community.

She has been in and out of hospital several times over recent months. Admissions were mainly due to panic attacks and shortness of breath and these were becoming more frequent and lasting for longer periods. When she was at home she would contact her GP about once a week. Across the system Marjorie was labelled as difficult and a nuisance. The GP asked the redesign team if they could help Marjorie, although at the time he didn't hold out much hope.

The team visited Marjorie in the Community Hospital where she had been transferred from the acute hospital some weeks earlier. Marjorie had been given eight weeks to live and told there was nothing more that could be done for her medically. Marjorie was steadfastly refusing to leave hospital – she couldn't see how she could manage alone at home and the prospect frightened her. The system was considering using formal processes to evict Marjorie to a residential home.

The team spent time with Marjorie to form a relationship with her and understanding what mattered to her most. They learned that she needed to feel listened to and be taken seriously. She was preoccupied with a pain in her ear, and was convinced she had a serious ear condition. She had previously asked for a scan but had been refused on the grounds that it wasn't medically necessary. The team quickly arranged a scan, which gave Marjorie the reassurance she needed. This was instrumental in building up the trust needed for Marjorie to open up about the things that really mattered to her.

Marjorie didn't want to be in hospital. She wanted to die at home but her greatest fear was dying alone, gasping for breath – hence the recent admissions for panic attacks and shortness of breath. It was important for her to feel reassured about her oxygen levels. It was also difficult to maintain contact with her friends and she was increasingly trying to do this via her mobile phone. There was no stimulation in hospital and she missed having good conversations and being able to access her DVD collection.

Marjorie also really wanted to be able to put her affairs in order herself before she died. Not being able to do this was making her stressed.

The team learned that she had a large aviary. She missed the birds and was very anxious about what would happen to them when she died. She also wanted to be able to enjoy her garden again but didn't believe this would be possible.

Having understood what mattered to her, the team began to explore practical solutions with Marjorie so that she felt more confident about going back home, supported by the team. They arranged for oxygen to be installed with a pulse oxygen meter so Marjorie could monitor her levels as many times a day as she wanted to. They helped her take control of her condition, monitor and control her medication. The support given to Marjorie was flexible and adjusted according to how she felt and what she needed on a day-to-day basis.

The team worked with a trusted friend to find good homes for the birds. It was agreed that the birds wouldn't be re-homed immediately, so that Marjorie could continue to enjoy them without worry.

Marjorie was able to maintain contact with her friends and to put her affairs in order. Finally, on a sunny day, Marjorie was able to sit in her garden with a cup of tea.

Jimmy and his Family

Jimmy was in receipt of a reduced disability benefit and was undergoing an appeal to try to claim the full benefit. He was injured some 14 years ago in a motorcycle accident and changes to the rules on benefits had impacted his eligibility to claim the full amount. The team supported him through his appeal, which he lost. He was then, of course, considered eligible for employment and for Job Seeker's Allowance (JSA). The team helped him to write his CV, look for jobs and to apply to a major supermarket chain as a checkout operator. He got the job on a part time basis and later accepted the offer of a full time role.

Jimmy had a difficult son, Richard, and two younger sons and there was considerable tension between the three boys and their parents. By working with the family the team identified a number of triggers which were caused by overcrowding. The team identified a more suitable property and was able to move the whole family quickly. At the same time Richard was supported in finding a suitable college placement designed to give him independent life skills. His attendance rose to 97% as opposed to 50% before the intervention.

Since the team started working with the whole family, demands on the police fell from nine calls per month to three calls over nine months. Each of these calls related to Richard's autism and the team is still exploring options to help him further. What this case shows is that peoples' problems are not isolated. The family needed help as a whole and the team needed the capability to recognise this and act accordingly.

~~~

Bill

One of the team in Stoke bumped into Bill by accident whilst working with another member of the community. He was 63 years old at the time and living alone; he was reclusive, isolated and with health issues. He was bordering agoraphobic. The outlook for Bill did not look great. In fact he was, in his words, 'marking time'.

The team worked with him to try to understand why he was so isolated. This involved building trust and some of the team tidied up his garden to encourage him to go outside, and bought him a garden bench to sit on. After a while the team managed to get him to go to the opticians to get his eyes tested. The reason he had not gone before was because he had lost his glasses and felt stupid about it. He also lacked the confidence to go alone. It was discovered he needed operations on both eyes which the team are now organising with his GP. The optician prescribed temporary glasses.

His confidence is now building and he is using the bus to get around, and has bought a dog for companionship. He is becoming self-supporting with some guidance and help from the team. If the intervention had not taken place its very likely that Bill would have either died alone or become a massive drain on the health service because his eye sight would have deteriorated to the extent that it could not be fixed.

Other authorities are also starting to experiment. Police forces are showing that it doesn't matter where you start, struggling people are struggling people wherever they hit the system.

Judy

When the police inspector responsible for a small town studied where demand for their police services was coming from, he learned that one woman had made more than a hundred calls for assistance over the last year. He had always had plenty of data about the calls but because she had used different phones on occasions, the calls had, over time, been classified in different ways by his staff. The classification suited his internal system and targets but gave no insight into the context of any given citizen. Not only did he not know how much of his officers' time was being taken up he didn't know what type of help this person needed.

Talking to members of his team who had been to see her on several occasions, he learned that she suffered from a condition that made her extremely sensitive to noise. She was currently housed in a flat with neighbours above, below and to either side, and was therefore frequently disturbed. Enquiries with the council noise department revealed that they also received a high number of calls from her, despite the fact that they had established that the noises were within acceptable levels – acceptable to the council that is.

Working with partners in the local housing association, it was possible to help the woman arrange a move to accommodation that was no more expensive but significantly less noisy. Her life was better, and time was freed up for the police officers.

The message should be simple and clear. The more you learn, the more you see how the current system racks up cost and failure and rarely solves the problems. The system defines the problem according to predetermined services and categories and if the citizen does not fit that definition (which is the norm) then the citizen remains in trouble and the wider system continues to spend money coping.

When you first read these examples it seems as though much time and effort is being spent on individual cases. The immediate reaction is that it cannot be affordable. But how much does it cost by not resolving these problems? A recent report from the BBC about the hard core of people presenting at A&E on a daily and weekly basis illustrates how long-term problems are not being given the right support. The consultant interviewed in the report told of people with drug, alcohol, mental health and loneliness problems. These are people who never fit into the services the system has designed and constantly fall between the cracks. The truth is that it is cheaper to help them directly than to continue providing the same old services.

It has been an eye-opener to see how government and public agencies inadvertently do more harm than good. For example, when I was working with police forces, officers would regularly give me examples of how the focus on 'detecting crime,' driven by government targets, succeeded in criminalising many people unnecessarily. Officers bemoaned, in particular, the criminalisation of many youngsters, thus blighting their lives. Similarly, drug treatment regimens have failed so badly that they have created a sense in users that they will never get off drugs. The current system disenfranchises us, albeit unwittingly, and often appears to make it as difficult as possible for citizens to go about their lives. Regulation such as money laundering, confidentiality and Criminal Records Bureau (CRB) checks make many simple things difficult. I see no evidence that HMG takes any steps to collect data around whether the regulation solves the problems it is intended to solve or whether the right problems were identified in the first place.

Government and public agencies will need to unpick the conditions (top-down procedures and practices) that have ensured that the system is too rigid to be of benefit to users. They need to make the necessary changes so that users can access what they need. The agencies should ask themselves and us, 'How well does the system work for the citizen and how do we know?'

Government will complain that we cannot be trusted and that regulation is important. We will have to collect the evidence over time. It is not about trust, it is about transparency – if we, the governed and the government, can see clearly what both parties actually do, and how they do it, then we wouldn't need to worry about trust. Regulation, for example, is important but it must be based on evidence that shows that regulation will overcome the problems. A security expert told me recently, for example, that money laundering regulation played no role in exposing money laundering and it certainly didn't stop the banks doing it – irony of ironies.

Stoke has discovered that people needing help are easy to find, easy to help and relatively few in number. We just have to learn to see them differently. It makes sense economically even if we do nothing other than help people over the crisis or problem that they face. The team in Stoke, however, found that once they had established trust by solving some immediate issues, people started to take responsibility for their own lives.

The message is simple: understand people in context and find out what matters to them. The solutions are then far easier and cheaper. It is not only cheaper to do this at the time but, because you build in resilience and help people take their own measures, it stays cheaper.

Chapter 2

Pull not push

In the UK today, by deciding what choices we ought to make, government and public sector agencies 'push' services at people, regardless of their actual needs. The notion of 'pull' – to be able to access what is actually needed – operates at many levels and requires service provision to be redesigned. It presupposes a number of things. First, and most importantly, it is based on the perception that the majority of citizens are responsible, in control of themselves, aware of what they need and able to make informed choices (Diagram 1, Chapter 1).

The idea of the 'responsible' citizen means that the system can change, from hunting for services that meet predefined needs to strengthening the citizen as a whole. The emphasis changes from supplying services to helping people look after themselves; in an ideal situation they would then only need to seek help in extremis. The first role of public agencies, then, would be to strengthen the community and create resilience and to support people's sense of responsibility for themselves. The second task would be to respond, to 'pull' the expertise needed to build in resilience from the wider system. This radically changes the role of the public agencies. They would no longer be the identifiers of need and designer of services. They would become supporters of communities and there to encourage communities to find and build on their strengths.

We can learn from Jim Diers[1] who has spent decades helping communities in Seattle to develop. Initially, he was helping interest groups with a particular problem or need, but as these groups became self-organising they worked with the city authorities to get support both in finance and expertise. The authorities learned to trust them and they learned to trust the authorities and the relationship between the two moved 180 degrees . The City was no longer designing and providing services but responding to requirements from the groups – 'pull'. This mutual trust was based on mutual knowledge of what each would and could deliver. For example, the groups had no means of managing their funds so the City acted as banker and treasurer. One of the most enduring and key elements was the agreement to put a value on the working time that volunteers contributed. The volunteers provided anything that was needed, from site clearance to professional and legal services. Diers

---

1 Jim Diers. (2004) *Neighbor Power: Building Community the Seattle Way*. Washington University Press

developed a system of matched funding – the notional value of the hours being matched by cash from the city. This way the groups had predictable and controllable income. They could not only pull for expertise but also for cash. The city found it a very cost-effective way of spending money. Not only were they spending less, but the money spent was being used well and achieving results that they could never have achieved alone. The time came when the number of groups had increased and then had to compete for resources. It would have been easy for the city authorities to behave as an arbiter. Instead, under Diers' guidance, they gave the arbitration job to the groups themselves: 'Get together, decide what is in the best interests of the geographic area as a whole and then agree what best fits in terms of your own interests.' The outcome was a very effective set of projects using fewer resources than if they had remained isolated interest groups.

The significance of Diers' work and that of others like him cannot be overstated. In his seminal work, *Bowling Alone: The Collapse and Revival of American Community*, Robert Putnam[2] analysed the evidence for community breakdown in America. He shows very clearly that many of the assumed reasons for the decline in public participation have been overestimated but there is one reason that does seem significant. What appears to account for most of the variation is the age group: older generations still contribute and engage in community activity but younger generations tend not to. It would be easy to accept this as a fact of life and that efforts to roll back the years will be wasted. Jim Diers, however, has shown that if something matters enough to people they will come together. The message is that we have to make it relevant.

An interesting accident happened in the Welsh Valleys. The local authority implemented its government Surestart policy by placing an office in a particularly deprived town. There was very little use for the Surestart programme but local people welcomed the office to help them solve problems. This is a good example of pull, although unintended!

Social services in Western Australia had a problem. Because communities are small, scattered and very difficult to serve from a centralised system, they decided to experiment – social workers were placed in small areas and told to see what worked for the citizens and for the department. The result was that the social workers developed a system that became known as Local Area Coordination (LAC), which has gone from strength to strength. The Local Area Coordinators (LACs) see themselves now as 'organisers' who seek to understand what matters to people and what problems they are really trying to solve. LAC seeks a local solution in the person's own social and geographic environs. So, for example, a woman caring for a child with severe learning problems

2 Putnam, R.. (2001) *Bowling Alone*. Simon & Schuster Ltd

needed to be able to do things herself and also have some respite. Her mother adored the child but lived very far away and it was too expensive to visit. Instead of providing expensive respite care (creating dependency as well as the usual problem of what happens when it's taken away at the next budget cut), they provided the petrol money for the grandmother to visit.

The focus is on building (and re-building) people's networks to allow and encourage them to be self-sufficient. An obvious question arises as to what happens when needs are more serious, but this simply creates a double layer of 'pull'. First, the person pulls the local coordinator who knows that the need is genuine. The coordinator then knows what to pull from the centre and the centre knows that the request is valid so there is no tedious 'eligibility' or validation required.

The results have been astonishing. Service perception has risen dramatically, despite the fact that people are getting far less than they would otherwise have received. The service started with a budget that by UK terms would be in the 'poverty ration' spectrum and very quickly demonstrated savings of 40%.

Canada and New Zealand have taken up the system. The UK is trying but too many people here see it as an alternative delivery mechanism without understanding the radical change of thinking from 'push' to 'pull'.

PLAN Canada, an organisation set up to help people with disabilities, found itself learning how to help people bend the rules to get funding. The government could have clamped down on this and tightened the rules, but instead it chose to study the problem and realised that people had little control over their funding, being dependent, as they were, on benefits. As the country's prosperity waxed and waned so did the state benefits. The answer that made best sense was a savings fund and they instituted the Canadian Federal Disability Savings Fund. This is a savings fund for citizens into which they can contribute money that will not be subject to means testing. It works on a graded basis. For less well-off people the government matches their savings dollar for dollar and for people with very few assets the government doubles any contribution they make. It has worked very well. People are now in control; they can carry the responsibility themselves and can pull from the system with confidence and certainty.

Stoke council has interpreted this logic and turned it into working practice. The teams work to a common purpose and set of principles. The purpose of the teams is to listen to what is meant by: *Help me to understand the problems in my life so that I can live my life well.* That purpose is then turned into action by a set of principles that guide what the teams do. At this stage, in order to have control and to be safe, most organisations would want to define procedures for staff to adhere to. But 'principles' prove to be a much better way to create focus and control.

Managers will have defined the principles using empirical data gathered through studying the demand in context and seeing what works. The principles are, therefore, operational, i.e. grounded in tangible things that can be carried out, not vague and woolly statements of 'value' or 'mission.' Managers can test the principles by asking, 'is what we've done true to the principle?' These are the principles they chose to define and work to:

Principle 1

I fully understand you and the real problems to solve.

This principle helps the team to understand that it is really important not to jump to conclusions about the help that citizens actually need. The focus is on building a relationship with each citizen and understanding life from his or her perspective. Building this relationship can take time and should not be rushed. It is during this time that the team member (or members) working with the citizen 'in context' starts to identify the real problems that need to be resolved if the citizen is going to rebalance his or her life. What is interesting is that, over time, it is possible to build a list of the most common and predictable demands that face citizens. The top twenty demands are shown in the table on the next page.

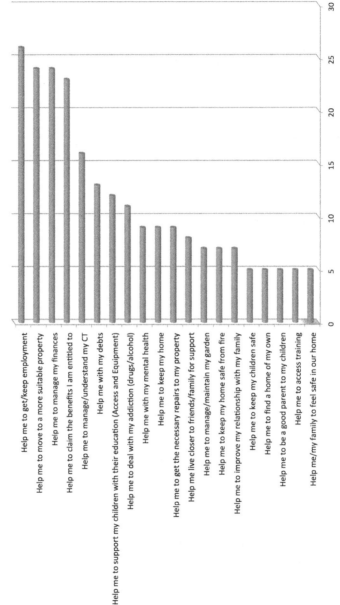

Demand in Context (Top 20 Demands) - frequency

Principle 2

I will help you to identify solutions to your problems.
There is no prescription for these solutions; the work needs to be designed as and when. Clearly the work isn't random in that, overall, people will have similar requirements. Support can be built empirically, based on the particular frequency and type of pull/problems to be solved in the location where you work.

Principle 3

I will help you to help yourself.
This is the outcome of the work and the goal that the process is working towards. How do we strengthen people and the people around them to sustain that better life?

Principle 4

We will 'Pull' in expertise when we need it.
As in 2) above, this is empirical. The expertise required will be defined over time by applying Principle 2 and Principle 3 above. Our work with clients has consistently shown that the expertise required is much less and far less varied than anyone could have predicted. The main requirements have been good listening and using ingenuity. Some specialist expertise will always be needed and is no less valuable but it supports individual need and, this is a hugely important point, because the expertise is being pulled the control is with the citizen and the team. This means that the team learns how that expertise can best be used, so it is much more adaptable. This is in stark contrast to the current system of experts who 'know best' and exert their own control (not their fault – that's what the system they work in requires of them). Also, in expert-driven push systems no-one apart from the expert, if anyone at all, learns anything.

Jane

In Bromsgrove a young single mother with an autistic child was experiencing rent problems and falling behind with other bills. The cause was pure disorganisation and pressure. Instead of penalising her they asked her what she wanted. She simply asked for some time and space to get herself organised. The team arranged two weeks respite after which she was back in control of her life.

There are many example of frontline people working to these principles, illustrating the simplicity of the work and the skills that are needed:

Tom

*A social services team in Somerset came across Tom. Tom was 90 at
the time, arthritic, hard of hearing and his vision was fairly poor. His
wife had dementia and was in a care home. His daily routine was
to get himself ready to go out, meet friends in town and do his daily
shopping before going to see his wife. He was a proud man and always
wanted to look his best.*

*He had an extensive social care package. He had recently had a fall.
This happened, almost inevitably, at a weekend and the ambulance
team attending had simply taken him to hospital where they diagnosed
a stroke because of Tom's slurred speech (due in reality to his poor
hearing). Tom eventually came out but much diminished by the
anxiety of not seeing his wife. A fortnight later, he fell again. Again it
was a weekend and the locum looked at the file, saw 'stroke' and sent
him straight to hospital. The team managed to get him out.*

*The team was determined to find out what mattered to Tom and
what was happening in his 'context'. They found that his daily routine
and his visit to his wife was what mattered most. His arthritis was
making it difficult for him to dress himself and was causing anxiety
and pressure for him. He also had a habit of putting his glasses on top
of his head, forgetting they were there and, when moving from room to
room, he was struggling to find light switches and falling over things.
The team 'pulled' the services of an innovative occupational therapist
who helped Tom solve his problems. She put Velcro on his shirts and
trousers, arranged for automatic light switches (motion detectors)
and made sure that the solutions worked for him. Tom was so pleased
it was all the team could do to stop him demonstrating his easily
removable clothing to all and sundry.*

This solution emerged from a combination of a full understanding of Tom
and the context of his life and then pulling the key skills to work with him
and discover solutions with him. It is essential to highlight that this was
not someone turning up and saying 'this is what you need' but someone
who took time to develop the solutions with Tom.

The care package was drastically reduced, Tom found much more
independence and confidence. The care workers were prepared to pull
whatever support Tom needed. It turned out that he needed very little.

In each of these two examples the people regained control and pulled
support for themselves. This is what is possible if there is mutual trust and
shows why that trust is so important. In Tom's example we have the local
support person providing that service.

The Co-production Movement

The Co-production Movement is based on the idea that the citizen and the agency can work with joint responsibility – 'work with', not 'do to'. The term co-production was originally used by Professor Elinor Ostrom of the University of Indiana to explain to the Chicago Police why crime went up when officers were taken off the streets and patrol cars were used instead. Her message was simply that citizens needed to work *with* the police.

Since then, Edgar Kahn, a civil rights lawyer in the US, has been mostly responsible for promoting co-production. He argues that neighbourhood support systems are vital, not just for the citizen but for the economy. The irony here is that you have to ask why it was ever anything else and just how far the public sector has moved to the 'expert, live your lives for you' model. Many social services and local authorities are beginning to experiment with co-production. Ruth Dineen, who has worked with Edgar Kahn, is pioneering a joined-up approach in Wales, with Welsh Assembly support. The test, as ever, will be whether they see it as a different way of thinking or simply a new process. Later in this chapter I give an example from the Beacon Hill estate in Falmouth that shows what can happen when people think differently about how to work with Local Authorities.

We have seen how the logic of 'pull' changes the function of the delivery organisation. But it has other radical consequences; the organisation becomes genuinely outward facing, taking its raison d'etre from the 'pull' of the citizen. The frontline teams become self-managing – they have everything they need: clarity of purpose, measures (is this what mattered to the citizen?) and principles (do what matters and be capable of doing what is pulled). The managers/leaders behind them still have purpose – to make sure that the system is capable of delivering what matters to citizens.

The dementia team in Monmouth stumbled into this by virtue of a manager who had the courage to do what mattered rather than what the system expected of him. The team had, until then, worked to the commissioned hours specified in the contract and to rotas worked out by administrators. The target was to keep capacity matched to commissioned hours. The manager realised that the driver for the work should be simply doing what mattered to the citizen and started to organise his team accordingly. The team members took to the task and took control, organising themselves around their new-found purpose.

Most would imagine that the hours would be out of control very quickly with considerable over-provision and lack of focus, but the result was that the hours worked stayed well in control, time was better used and service quality improved dramatically (from something that had not been particularly bad in the first place). They have now created excess capacity to the point where they are negotiating definitions with the social services team as there are not enough people classified with dementia to meet their new-found capacity. They are now accepting people who are simply less capable than they were. Unsurprisingly, the skills and activities used by the team are just the same – listening effectively to people and their families as well as rebuilding relationships within the community.

The transformation stemmed from the fact that the team had clear purpose – do what matters and work to clear principles. (It's important that people choose principles that reflect their work and that describe what 'good work' means to them. The overall sense of the principles will be broadly similar across situations.)

The principles they chose for the project are as follows:

- Care cannot be provided without establishing a relationship with the person receiving care.
- No uniforms.
- The emotional and social needs of the people supported are as important as their physical needs.
- The needs of the informal carer (usually a family member) must not only be assessed but met.
- Decisions are best made by those closest to the issues and we must trust our staff.
- There must be a direct dialogue between the care coordinator and the team.

I quote from one evaluation report prepared by the team:

> M came home from hospital; not eating, drinking or communicating. She had lost all ability to walk, had short term memory loss and her will to carry on had gone. M was under 5 stone, prone to chest infections and malnourished.
>
> M has a devoted daughter and refused to let her 'Ma' give up. There had been other agencies visiting M so we were just another agency. She had formed an opinion, ready to do battle after what she says was appalling care in hospital.
>
> After our care, M's lust for life returned. We sit and eat with M which the family likes. M enjoys cooked meals, pudds, cuppas, chocolate. M now goes out on Wednesdays, tea dance on Thursdays. M sings along with us, dances with her arms; loves touching, hugging us and communicating. She enjoys her music at home, has visitors and enjoys the socials with Friends of Dingestow where she meets old friends and neighbours – connecting with the community.
>
> Something her family never thought would be possible was for her to attend her only granddaughter's wedding with our support. Her daughter says she has never experienced care like it.

The team decided what each person needed and negotiated with each other to make the time and resources available. Every member of the team 'owned' their citizens and therefore made sure that what was needed was available. As noted earlier, they worked with local people to re-establish networks, both for support and for social engagement. Here is another quote from the report:

> The [dementia] team has established two [geographical] groups, Friends of Raglan and the Friends of Dingestow. These two groups are voluntary, local networks supported by but not run by the dementia team. The control is thus with the community not with the experts.

The support from the team, therefore, tended to be 'little and often' and became flexible and easier to manage. An example from their report:

> Mr M now feels confident to administer his own medication and we have encouraged and assisted Mr M to cook and he has taken a keen interest again in this task. He is attending tea dances again now that J has attended with him to regain confidence. He now calls on neighbours whom he feels are vulnerable to encourage them to attend the socials at Dingestow. He has a purpose and a spring in his step. His care had reduced from 7 hours to just 15 minutes per week.

It is not likely that any manager could have designed that system directly – it evolved through the team's own control. In parallel, absenteeism and labour turnover, both of which had been high, dropped to zero. This is how staff talk now, as quoted in the report:

> "I feel the pressure has been lifted off my head. I don't worry about my wages every month and I'm not worrying when my rota arrives."

> "I feel excited about my job; my daughter said she has never heard me talking about work so much – just loving it. I put my whole heart into work."

Also, the care prevented many of the people from having to visit hospital, and reduced GP visits. This not only saved the system significant cost but maintained the stability, comfort and longevity of their charges. A longer better life and a better death are indeed realities.

Compelling evidence for this comes from Atul Gawande, in his 2014 Reith Lectures based on his book, *Being Mortal*[3]. Gawande is an American physician who has made careful studies of the impact of medicine, as it is currently practised, on people's lives, not just on their health. He describes how physicians are keen to do what they believe matters from a medical perspective but in ignorance of what matters to people as people rather than as patients. He quotes an MIT study that took a group of terminally ill lung cancer sufferers. The study divided the people into two groups.

---

3 Atul Gawande. (2014) *Being Mortal*. Profile Books

Both groups received the full medical care that was appropriate. One group, however, was asked what mattered to them, what they wanted to do with the time they had left and how they wanted to plan their death. The result was that this group asked for 30% less medication, often forgoing chemotherapy, spent 30% less time in hospital and lived 25% longer than the other group. Psychologically what has happened here is that for the first group the medical system is in control but the second group has been given back responsibility for their own life (and death).

The exciting thing for the public agencies is that the logic of 'pull' creates focus – and confidence in that focus. Dealing with people case by case, in terms of what matters to them and what they can be helped to do for themselves clarifies the role of the supporting organisation. For most of the people that the Stoke team helped, for example, the common denominator was financial problems due to people being unemployed. This is empirical evidence across the cases that they have worked with. This has given the chief executive the confidence to spend time and money (which will accrue from the savings created by the new approach) on creating jobs, knowing that it will have a big impact on the system and the citizens. The same logic applies to communities. Just as we ask of the citizen: 'What would a good life look like for you?' we ask of the community: 'What would make this a good place to live?

Green, Moore and O'Brien have been developing what they call Asset Based Community Development (ABCD) in the USA. They work to the same principles of finding and building strengths (assets). Their book, *When People Care Enough to Act*[4], provides a useful handbook for community activists. The authors talk about seeing the problems from the community point of view. I quote, 'If the community thinks it has a rat problem, it probably has a rat problem'. In this case the authorities helped the community solve their own rat problem and, in doing so, helped them to realise how they could work together to improve their neighbourhood further. However, their examples are not exclusively 'pull'. They engage in one 'push' activity and that is to select and train community activists.

They have been doing ABCD for some years and are able to show extraordinary successes. One example is a rundown ghetto in a city suburb in the deep south. Everything that we would say was inevitable existed there: urban decay, drugs, loss of businesses, shabby and empty property. This US suburb was worse than anything they might have classified as beyond help. Yet, some community activists pulled people together, built trust with their fellow citizens, organised working parties and, in partnership with the city authorities, transformed the suburb into a thriving, attractive, fresh and modern place to live. That City authority now has confidence in knowing that the right amount of money is doing the right thing.

---

4 Green, Moore, O'Brien (2007) *When people care enough to act.* Inclusion Press

An example of this kind of activist training was exemplified in the UK in Falmouth. The Beacon and Old Hill estate was a severely run-down area. The regeneration started with training and support for a small group of opinion leaders in, for example, how to apply for grants. The group proved itself to the local authority as capable and reliable and a formal partnership was set up with local agencies. This in turn, as in Seattle, changed the relationship with the local authority. I quote from a report (which I reference in Chapter 5):

> The effect of the formation of this Partnership, not least in terms of the trust which it built up in the authorities, was a noteworthy break in the traditional working practices of local government. Rather than maintaining sole control of the budget and decision making processes, Carrick District Council agreed to delegate some of its powers, a process which empowered the Partnership, which remained a predominantly tenant-led body, rather than a council committee, to make recommendations to the full council concerning the estate's progress. As Mike Owen, Senior Housing Officer for Carrick District Council at the time, said: "It was quite brave for the authority to extend responsibility to a body controlled by residents." While the decision may indeed have been brave, it had the effect of ensuring that it was the specific local needs of the community which were being responded to, with local, directed, changes being the result. Perhaps the most poignant expression of this localisation of the decision making progress is to be found in the way that the Partnership worked together with the tenants to determine the order of priority for the improvement work on the buildings enabled by the award of the Capital Challenge funding. Such localised self-organisation in turn ensured that, for the community as a whole, there was clear evidence of the fairness of the prioritisation of the re-cladding and heating improvement work to be undertaken.

Note that this did not result from a planned process. The change in relationship was emergent – as the community learned to trust the authorities and the authorities learned to trust the community, solutions emerged from the new relationship. It was iterative. The more they worked together, the more they saw mutual possibilities, and the more they experimented to find what could work.

It's a simple logic that has been demonstrated in so many places. Portsmouth City Council paid attention to fly tipping and graffiti in their social housing areas and the community responded by engaging in solving anti-social behaviour issues and many other community issues.

In the late 60s there was an innovative project in Newcastle which gave rise to the Byker Estate. The local community, people who had been living in the terraced homes that were demolished to make way for the estate, was consulted on the design and it was hailed as groundbreaking architecture. Since then the estate has gone through cycles of problems and regeneration. The problem seems to be that it has never become a mainstream idea – the supporting system has not been properly developed. Locals are reported as having become thoroughly fed up with people visiting it as they would a freak show. The latest effort has led to a Multi Agency Approach. Once again we have the idea of working together but not differently – the thinking did not change. As the debate continues about whether the Byker Wall should be listed continues, it is still being viewed as architectural innovation more than social. The community lessons seem to have to be learned over and over again. We should ask why. Why is it that sound economic and social progress remains a fringe activity? What does it take to listen to and understand people in context, both as individuals and communities – to pay attention to what matters, help them solve the pressing problems, build networks (that's what a community is) and relationships, to become more resilient and less needy?

A recent report in the UK recommended that Her Majesty's Government (HMG) should stop regeneration investment in many northern towns as there was no evidence of any improvement. This should not be seen as a social statement but a failure of method. It is a result of the self-defeating 'push' methodology – the 'we know best' approach.

Meanwhile back in the USA, another eye-catching example from Green, Moore and O'Brien's work was that of a woman who decided to 'end poverty' in her neighbourhood. Apart from the ambitiousness of it, you would have to wonder how on earth she went about it?' Well, she simply started a community 'venue' and invited people from all walks of life, from business leaders to down and outs, and started by helping them to get to know each other. There were rules and principles to the venture, but the outcome over time was that people were offered jobs by people they knew and with whom they now had a relationship.

For me this is the recurring theme – networks and relationships. Build and strengthen these and communities will tell you what they need, especially as they will have such a trusting relationship with their municipal and public agencies.

The message is clear. Help people learn how to take control of their own lives, their networks and communities and then develop a pull system that responds to responsible needs. It is very affordable and you know the money is well spent – targeted at things that are going to work – by design.

Chapter 3

Expertise not Services

If citizens are encouraged to take responsibility for themselves then the role of the 'service provider' changes dramatically.

There are two main considerations: what support is needed by the citizen and who provides it? The 'what' is now an empirical issue: the citizen and citizen groups learn what they need. As they learn, they will seek support, and as they find out what works and learn more about their own and their provider's competencies, a clear picture will evolve.

The Seattle experience provides a good example of its evolution. In the first instance, the groups needed information on how to do things – how to manage the legalities of land use and corporate bodies, how to build things, how to manage group events and engage people. They also found that they needed to manage the flow of money. The City authority, therefore, found that its role was to meet these particular needs. They provided the banking facilities as well. This was not a reactive process. The role of the City 'experts' became one of consultant, working with the groups, helping them shape their learning and pulling the support needed from the relevant offices. Both learned together, building trust and confidence. The authority found it most helpful to open a small office in the community that acted as the contact point and meeting place. The most important thing was for the authority to use the office as a learning site – understanding the demand and making sure that the people staffing it had the capability to respond competently.

The confidence of the provider is every bit as important as the confidence of the citizens. Citizens do not necessarily know what they don't know and experts need to adopt a significant consultancy role in helping citizens to understand what will work best. Thus the normal relationship – where the municipal agency defines the need, designs the service and measures the delivery – is reversed. Citizens define what they need and pull accordingly. The measure of whether it works is self-defining – either it works for the citizens or it doesn't.

A UK police force started to operate a 'pull' system. Their traditional structure was local neighbourhood and response units with centralised specialist teams, such as major investigations, firearms and forensics. In an experiment, the central teams were put on 'standby' to see how often they would be needed. After six months only one unit, forensics, had been pulled from the specialised teams.

What the police learned was that by working alongside the forensics team they understood more about the work they did. Forensic utilisation became more efficient as the frontline teams only pulled their expertise when they knew it was going to make a difference. Both developed confidence in each other and the number of times forensics contributed to the success of an investigation went up. This 'pull' method is in stark contrast to a previously procedural approach where the centre decided the criteria that required forensics to attend. What the force learned calls into serious question the way government has outsourced forensics to private agencies. The contractual cost-per-job system would undermine this work. Unit costings encourage people to pay attention to what is specified not necessarily what matters. The contract should pay attention to effectiveness of outcome and overall cost rather than activity.

What, therefore is the role of 'expertise'? In the first place it is the giving of expert information and advice. In the second place, it is the provision of expert skills, i.e. doing things the citizen or frontline teams cannot do for themselves. It is also this notion of working with citizens to educate, learn with and understand requirements and solutions. Thus the third role of expertise is to ensure that the system learns, grows and adapts.

A Somerset GP worked closely with the local social care team to experiment with care for the chronically ill, most of whom were older people. Together they selected a team comprising professionals whose expertise would be expected to be of value. For the most part, as they visited patients, the team actually required little more than good listening skills, a bit of ingenuity and lateral thinking. They discovered that the 'professional' approach could get in the way and stifle the best solutions. Interestingly the Occupational Therapist was often the source of the solutions but it could have been any one of the team. One element of expertise they certainly needed was that of the pharmacist. Many of the problems they found were with the prescribed drugs and how they were or were not being used by the people they were visiting. The irony here is that the pharmacist was surgery-based and the one person not included in the team. The experiment is ongoing and it remains to be seen whether the pharmacist's knowledge will be used to re-design the way the GPs prescribe and support drug use or whether the pharmacist remains an important consideration in the make-up of the visiting team.

It is an important distinction. The expertise needed to create change and establish the new regime may not be the expertise needed to keep it running. Once again, this is an empirical question – learn by doing.

The team in Stoke found that alcohol problems featured consistently amongst the people they worked with. They quickly added an 'alcohol' expert to the group who now works directly with people rather than forcing them to go through assessment and referral processes. The results have been impressive. The treatment has taken place in the context of the people's lives and families, and has been far more meaningful and productive. It is no longer seen as an 'alcohol problem' but as part of a process of getting someone back to a good life. As the citizens who have been helped become more confident in their ability to stay clear of alcohol they naturally become more confident in themselves and are then able to do other things.

Learning by doing is not just knowing the expertise to call on but the experts also learn how best to use their skills. The real added bonus of this process is that the rest of the team learn as well. In a traditional system, even when the expertise is well used, no-one else learns much. In this case, the team learns not only what the expert can do but it learns that much of what the expert does was not that complicated, and some of the skills they could easily learn themselves. They, therefore, also learn when the expert is needed.

The expertise required can also be that of making connections. There are many people doing good things already but in the transactionalised and disconnected system today there is no obvious way of finding them. A project in Gloucestershire looking after older people started work through a local charity with a good reputation. The charity was, as ever, the work of a particularly enthusiastic and creative individual. She had created, among other things, a very good community network and had ready options for many needs. In particular, however, she worked with a small organisation called Care and Repair. It was already well connected with the local authority but as a traditional service. It was not until they looked at the service in the context of the project that they realised how innovative and useful it was.

There was an apparently similar service offered by Age UK that provided cleaning, shopping and maintenance. The difference was that Care and Repair offered a brokerage service which simply, but importantly, connected people who needed help to local people who offered it. The citizen had the relationship with the maintenance person rather than, as with Age UK, the organisation. It was thus a trust relationship and much cheaper without a middle man.

It will also be the case that the teams working with citizens will have to 'pull' expertise from other agencies who have not been directly involved in the work. The key is to present clear case histories including the full story and probable cause and effect – the full impact of what the current system has done and is doing. A good example from Bromsgrove will serve to illustrate this. The local prison governor was concerned at the lack of support for prisoners, and the way in which the current system predicted that released prisoners would end up back in the system. He became interested in the work one of the teams was doing. The team and the governor took the case of one young prisoner due for release. He had missed out on much of his formal education and saw that a future lay in acquiring qualifications. The team approached the local college and negotiated a placement for him. They also found him somewhere to live to give him the basic security of a home. The result was exemplary and the young man's life is on the way to a sustainable turnaround.

It is worth re-emphasising that this chapter has not been about agencies working together but about agencies working and thinking differently. In most cases they have done that as a consequence of getting involved with the communities and citizens and learning how to respond to what matters.

Chapter 4

Using data

There are two decisions to be made when using data – what data to collect and how to make use of it.

Pioneers of the new way of thinking understand that data must reflect context. If the purpose is to change people's lives through understanding them in their context, the data needs to show how well that is being achieved. The current system simply looks at transactions out of context. For example, the telephone centres for the NHS (NHS Direct, as was, and now 111) measure call-answering times, duration of calls and resolution from the call centre's perspective. What they don't address is why someone has called and how best to resolve that type of problem. They don't measure how many people didn't need to call. Or what is happening in the rest of the system that does not work. It is no accident that NHS Direct became known as NHS Redirect – resolution would routinely mean 'passing it on'.

How to choose the data you need

The new approach to data collection pays attention to how good the system is at understanding issues at first presentation. It shows whether the right thing was done at the first point of contact – either by resolving it or designing the right course of action and setting it up to happen. The data then tracks the process from the citizen's point of view, to see how well and how quickly lives are stabilised and/or improved sustainably.

The Stoke team uses a spider diagram (*Figure 1*) to plot the outcomes for each person.

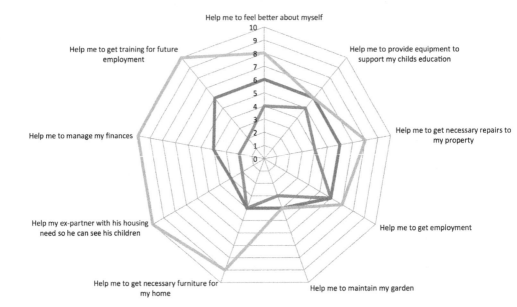

Figure 1

The inner grey line shows their starting position, the middle grey line shows progress after three months and the outer pale grey line shows progress three months later. They are, in essence, a set of self-reporting rating scales showing how much progress has been made on the question, 'How well have the actions taken worked for me?' The ratings are taken over time to see progress.

The team quickly discovered, as mentioned earlier, that after initial support people develop more confidence and sort their own problems out. Reviewing the outcome and keeping the information on what it was that was done or not done to improve a situation helps support people to measure what needs to be learned. For example:

- Are we solving the problems?
- Are we solving the problems in the most effective way (time and impact) and could we find a better method?
- How much is it costing us overall to achieve these results?

It would be tempting to use a question like the following as a measure: 'How well are we doing on alcohol and mental health?' However this would probably take us back to the problem of seeing issues out of context and, worse, create campaigns for alcohol and/or mental health.

The question of the success or failure of the methods used is vital. Only by collecting data and comparing method across cases, across time, across practitioners and across locations can we learn. The team at Stoke kept a record of everything done, case by case, in order to correlate the results and to test both method and what actually worked. The team also aggregated the issues from their citizens (as in Chapter 2). The primary purpose of the aggregation was to identify the skills needed for the work rather than to put labels on the issues.

As an approach to measurement the team developed three different levels of data:

- the impact on the individual
- the impact on the neighbourhood
- the impact on the whole system.

As the team developed the work, they began to see common patterns that occurred amongst the people they were trying to help. The indicators that were most diagnostic were:

- having rent arrears greater than £100
- having council tax arrears
- having been involved in crime or anti-social behaviour
- having been referred to the Children's and Young People's service for issues such as school attendance.

These indicators represent what happens to families who are struggling. What they do not tell you is what has caused these problems. The work with each family builds a picture of the consistent problems and the indicators give an idea of the scale of the problems, which in turn allows the team to predict the likely type and amount of resource they will need to help the individual or family.

Based on these same indicators the team could identify the numbers of households in the neighbourhood or ward that fitted the pattern, which in turn allowed them to make a crude estimate of the need for support by the authorities. They developed a Triangle of Need (*Figure 2*) to identify the percentage of households in crisis (T1), the percentage in need of some support (T2) and the percentage needing no support(T3).The Triangle of Need gave at least some sense of the scale of the task. The work itself is likely to validate the estimates. Over time it will be helpful to collect comparative data from similar families who have not been helped and the amount of resources they need and from families who have already reached a crisis state. This should allow the team to measure the impact of improving the lot of the families and also what will have been saved by preventing them from going into crisis.

As it stands, the team estimates that 28% of households are likely to benefit from support. Using the same indicators but at more extreme values, e.g. evictions, more serious crime, school exclusions, the team estimated the number of households in crisis to be around 6%. The remaining 66% of households were not considered in need of support. It is worth reiterating that this is not intended to be definitive data but a way to give some idea of the scale of work and the money and resources that might be needed.

In the diagram below the figures are the numbers of households and the percentage of the total households that are estimated to be in each of the three levels. This framework enabled the Stoke team to understand who they needed to work with and the impact they were having on the wider system.

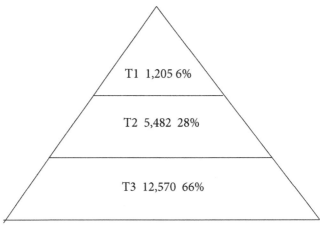

Figure 2 – Triangle of Need

Below are some of the measures that can be used to describe the impact on neighbourhoods and the wider system. The first graph, *Figure 3*, shows that notices to evict social housing tenants reduced when tenants were helped to manage themselves and their finances. The second graph (*Figure 4*) shows how anti-social behaviour (ASB) reduced during the same period, and the third graph (*Figure 5*) shows how total crime reduced.

As the work is extended to other wards and more work is tested, then the authorities will want data from across the city on similar things, e.g. crime levels, health attendance and school attainments in order to gauge the impact on the wider system.

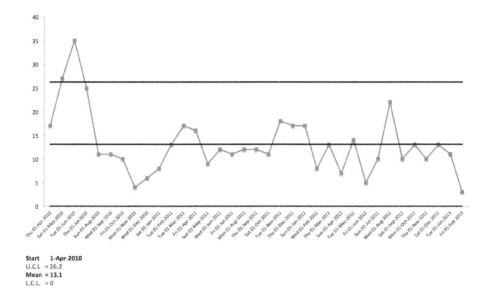

Figure 3: Evictions from social housing

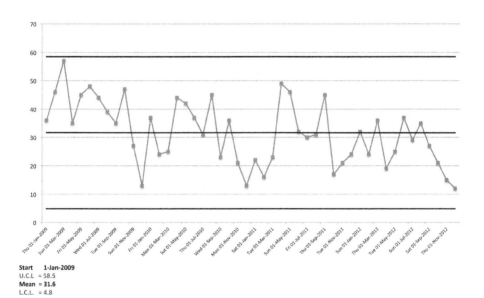

Figure 4: Incidents of ASB

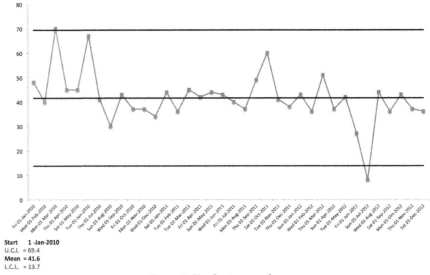

Start   1 -Jan-2010
U.C.L = 69.4
Mean = 41.6
L.C.L = 13.7

Figure 5: Total crime numbers

Leading and Lagging Indicators

One of the most important things to understand when using data is the difference between leading and lagging indicators. The leading indicator is the one that you should pay attention to. It is the one that you seek to understand and learn about. A lagging indicator is one that takes care of itself if you have improved the leading indicator. For example, if we learn about what matters to people and improve that (a leading indicator) then their health probably improves and they spend less time in hospital or make fewer visits to the GP (a lagging indicator). Monmouth social services, for example, have halved the number of people who contact them and receive a statutory care package; they have halved the number of people who go into residential care and reduced by a third the number of hours they spend with each citizen – for the right reasons. These are all lagging indicators. The leading indicator that they paid attention to was what mattered to each citizen who contacted them. (They have saved £1.5m in the process.)

Equally, if we understand who criminals are, why they do what they do (leading) then we will catch more of them and the crime rate will go down (lagging). At the moment police forces track crime (lagging indicator). It is very difficult to correlate actions they have taken with specific reductions in crime. The only action that appears to have made a significant difference is preventative measures relating to household and vehicle security – things in which the police would have been tangentially but not directly involved. The leading indicators – what they should pay attention to – are the causes of crime, who the criminals are, how they get to be that way and what they do. Thus, when crime prevention measures make burglary more difficult they will know and predict what the burglars will do instead.

The spider diagrams and the 'indicators of need' developed by Stoke are leading indicators. If we do the same, we can pay attention to what matters to people and learn how to identify people who need help. We can test the data and the measurement regime. It is doing its job if it helps us improve people's lives. This is the primary test of a correct measure. If it is not improving lives then it is an incorrect measure. Leaders must keep applying this test. Their job is to help frontline teams make this assessment by constantly asking how well the data is helping to improve lives in a sustainable way.

The other test of a correct measure is that it is owned by the teams doing the work. It is not management data as we currently know it. Leaders will be interested in it but it is frontline data, developed by the front line because it shows them that they are doing good work and armed with that data they will know how to do more of what works and less of what does not. A useful way forward for leaders, therefore, is to say, 'How do we know what works? Show me the data'.

The leading indicators, the data that we should pay attention to first of all, are at the personal level: what matters to individuals, how well we understand it and how well we are doing in solving the issues for citizens and strengthening them in their lives. If we do that well, there should be positive consequences at community and geographical levels and it will show in the lagging indicators – crime rates, rent arrears, homelessness and other population data. We will need this consequential data – the outcomes that matter – but it is vital to understand that it takes care of itself if we get the personal data right. The big mistake that the current system makes is to manage the system by outcome data. The data isn't wrong, it's just used wrongly. If you manage systems by outcome data then you invite people to distort it. If you want to reduce waiting times at hospitals you have to understand why individuals are attending hospitals and how to solve those problems case by case, then the waiting times will fall as a consequence. If you manage the system by waiting time data then people will distort the system to fit the data. Hospitals are also very good at collecting data about average length of stay and seek to reduce that as a measure of their effectiveness. What they do not collect is data that says how many days in total any given patent spends in a hospital over any period of time – in other words, how often, and for how long, they come back in. In one hospital we found that a small core of patients was re-admitted with frightening regularity. The staff were shocked to realise the truth. The leading data should have been about why people were admitted.

Length of stay is a lagging indicator and was teaching them nothing. The lagging data is the impact on the system – for example, the graphs earlier in this chapter that show the reduction in ASB and crime.

This then is the pattern. Use personal data to get knowledge. As you build knowledge, possible solutions will become more and more obvious. Experiment and learn what works and then relate the learning to the outcomes to ensure that the system works.

A recent example from Utah is remarkable. People studying homelessness tracked the impact of homelessness on individuals and saw the pattern of consequences both to the individuals and to the costs of all the various agencies – crime, health, education, etc. What became obvious was how crucial it was for individuals to have a stable home – somewhere secure to live. So, they decided that they would experiment with providing a free home to all homeless people. The solution was not the free home; the solution was helping people attain some stability. Over time they have found that the free home has become the best lever for achieving stability. While most people have been helped to help themselves, some continue to have problems. Overall, though, it is still cheaper to give all homeless people a free home than to deal with the consequences of a lack of stability. If they had started with cost and outcome data they would never have arrived at that solution. The goal would have been to reduce cost and, as in the UK, the method would have been to reduce benefits.

The pattern is clear again. Study individual cases to get knowledge. Use that knowledge to generate data. Use that data to run experiments and then see what impact it has on the outcomes that matter to the population and to your organisation.

Let's look at another example, a police system. Greater Manchester Police suffered the brutal murder of two officers by a local gang leader and mounted an operation to crack down on gangs in the city. They then had the foresight to attempt to find out what caused people to become gang members. An excellent piece of research led by a senior officer discovered that there was a strong relationship between being subject to and seeing domestic violence as a child and becoming a gang member. This knowledge provides all sorts of productive opportunities for experimenting with solutions as well as methods to guide the policing activity itself. There is no knowing at this stage what will work but there is plenty of opportunity for collecting good data on method. The leading indicators will be around causes of domestic violence and the outcome (lagging) data will be around reduction in violence, crime and possibly many other things. This contrasts with a well-intended but wrong-headed government initiative to increase prosecutions for domestic violence (lagging data). This tended only to drive the violence underground and generated no useful knowledge of any merit. In fact, prior to the initiative and following yet another child death scandal, forces were encouraged to focus on child protection. Previously most forces had had family protection teams where child protection and domestic violence went hand in hand. The focus on child protection and then domestic violence had the unwitting consequence of ensuring that the system learned as little as possible about either. The child protection teams had no knowledge of the families who were being followed for domestic violence, and vice versa.

Until the system has changed we need to run the new and the old measures together. This is not as complicated as it sounds in that most of the old (current) measures are simply lagging measures – cost, numbers of incidents (rent arrears, pot holes, crime detections) and the like. It is important to run the two together so that we can understand with confidence that when we pay attention to the leading measures, the lagging measures do indeed reduce in the right way. So, for example, many local authorities we work with are discovering that by paying attention to leading indicators, such as why people want social housing (asking them what problem they want to solve) and why people want to move within the social housing system, the lagging indicators, like demand for social housing, drops dramatically (lagging indicators).

One of the most important lagging indicators to track is cost. I have made the point several times that to manage by cost is to create problems but it must still be tracked. What you will be tracking, though, is the cost end to end rather than transaction costs.

The examples I have described in this book are saving a lot of money but we are only just beginning to understand how much, where and when. What is clear, though, is that if we pay attention to *value* rather than *cost,* costs come down. We learn how to do only but exactly what matters and it only gets done once, preventing failure downstream.

The need for accountability remains, however; we need to know how public money is being spent. We also need to know how best to make savings and how to allocate finances across all systems. The current budgeting system remains problematic in that action in one area (e.g housing) can save money elsewhere (e.g police and health) and so a more integrated budgeting system needs to be developed.

How to use data to learn over time

Another key part of collecting data is how to represent it. You will notice that the data in the diagrams above has been collated in run-chart form, so that the changes over time are clear. This is very important. The technique is called Statistical Process Control (SPC) and is designed to help you learn about your system. Let's take a simple example. I work in a call centre and you are my manager. You notice (*Figure 6* below) that the number of calls I take varies from day to day. You want me to take 80 calls a day overall. On Monday I take 100 but on Tuesday I only take 60. I only take 60 on Wednesday as well so you might be concerned enough to pay attention to my performance. What would you say? 'Everything alright Richard? Everything alright at home?' If my performance then goes up to 100 again on Thursday you will probably feel you've done the right thing – 'nipping it in the bud'.

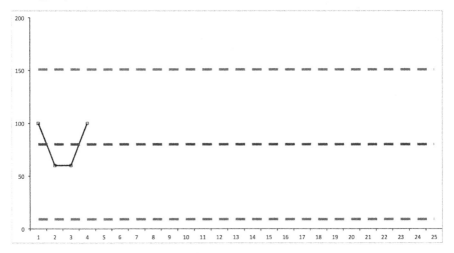

Figure 6 : Performance over 4 days

– – – – control lines
– – – – average number of calls

What *is* wrong, however, is that you pay attention to me at all. Why does my performance vary? Typically, it is due to a variety of things: the time I spend on the phone, how much I know, the capability of the IT system and the type of calls I am taking. If I am new, then I have not yet learned the short cuts in the system or I have not yet learned how to cheat to make my targets. If I am new, each call is quite stressful. As I try to learn about the system as well as help the caller I need more breaks and spend less time at the my desk. If I take a difficult call is there someone there to help? The reasons for the variation are not really down to me but are down to features of the system of work: training, supervision, how easy or complicated the call system is, etc. It doesn't matter, then, what target you set me, I can only do what I can do. If we apply some basic statistics that show the normal variation (*Figure 7*) then what becomes obvious is the typical level and range of performance that you can expect as a consequence of the system I work in.[1]

---

1 For more information on how control charts are created and their interpretation please see, Guilfoyle, S (2013) p63–72

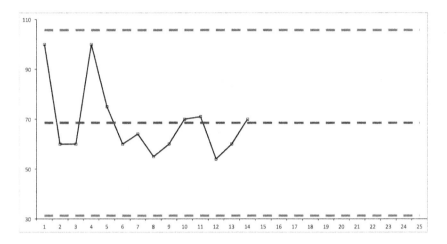

Fig 7: Normal variation for a particular piece of work

It shows the actual average of my performance (in this case 68) over a period of time as opposed to any target I might have been set. My performance can now be predicted and you can expect broadly the same next week and the week after. If you want me to perform better and take more calls then you have to change the system: design a better call system, make the service better so that people do not have to call in with difficult problems, etc. The charts are the lagging indicators that show you what happens. The task is to pay attention to the leading indicators – how I manage calls and what causes me to take shorter or longer calls. The charts will then show whether or not that attention works. If it works then the average goes up but also the range, i.e. the variation will reduce as I become more consistent and the features that caused the variation have less impact. You will know immediately whether or not what you have done has changed the system and not just caused a temporary blip.

For example, I worked with a private healthcare company where the operator had to set up customer details on two systems, one that logged the treatment provider and one that logged the customer's contact details. The standard training specified the sequence whereby that should be done. By studying the high performers we found that one operator had discovered for herself that if she reversed the standard options she could dramatically reduce the talk time and improve the service. The average talk time was around four minutes but her talk time was around two and half minutes. When we transferred her learning to everyone, performance improved across the system (*Figure 8*). Because the charts show time and variation we could see the difference and we knew it was down to the change we had made. This gave everyone the confidence of knowing what had worked and that it was worth doing more of it. Equally, if you make a change and it does not make a difference to the chart, however plausible it may have been, you know that it is not worth persevering with.

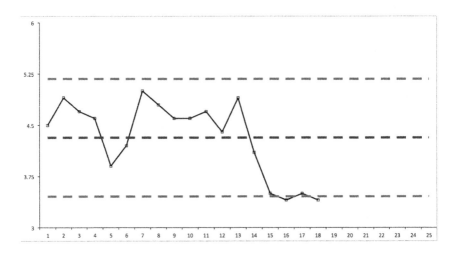

Figure 8

The graph can be split to show that it is now a different system and predictably so:

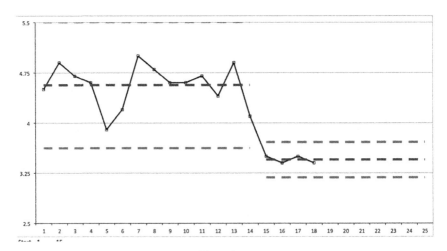

Figure 9

In most systems today, averages are the main measures used. All you see is the statement of averages as opposed to the variation around the average that is so important. It's hard to describe just how misleading this is. It's the old joke of the man who drowned in a river that on average was two feet deep or, as one commentator put it, the man who had his head in the oven and his feet in the fridge but on average was quite comfortable.

The run charts with the statistics applied are called control charts. You do not need to be a statistical expert to produce them as there are many easy programmes that will do it for you. It is essential, however, that you put your data into these charts so that you are certain about what is happening. Your goal is to know what the steady system can produce and to know that when you make changes they make a difference and that that difference is sustainable – over time. So, for example, the chart below (*Figure 10*) is taken from the work done by a social services team in South Wales that worked hard to help people when they first contacted the department. In the original system, the person's details would be taken and an appointment made for an assessment before doing the work. This had taken 30 days on average and anything up to 90 days as a matter of routine. Over the period of four months you can see how their efforts transformed the system and the norm now is assessment on day one. More importantly, they can see that their efforts are succeeding and they know what to do more of and what to do less of.

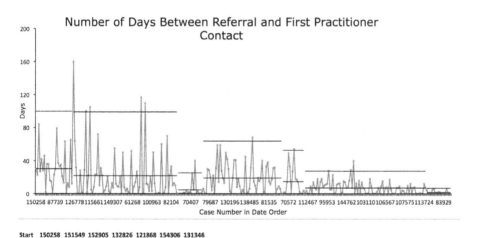

Figure 10

The control lines above and below the mean represent normal distribution. For example, we learn that normal distribution for the height of a male in Britain is between 5'4": 6'2" and you would not give a second glance to anyone within that height range. If they were taller or shorter then you might notice. Equally, it becomes more probable that any height outside that range is due to unusual causes. So, in practice the control lines describe 90+% of the data and you can be reasonably confident that anything within the lines is down to the day-to-day operation of your system – stuff that happens all the time. Anything outside the lines is probably something different. In the call centre, it might be a Monday when people are calling in to resolve issues they could not resolve over the weekend or it might be due to a promotion or a new form that has been sent out. It might have been a system problem. These are not daily occurrences. You may not need to act on them but you will need to understand them. For example, if you see the call levels that occur when a new form is sent out you may want to pay attention to how forms are designed or whether a form was the best way to have helped the customer in the first place.

In many systems when you first look at them you find that the lines are quite spread apart and many data points lie outside those lines. This tells you that there is a lot of variation in the system and that it is not under control. It is very difficult to manage such a system and many people will be wasting a lot of time trying to improve it and probably getting the blame for poor performance. Understanding your system and eliminating causes of variation that have been designed in (measuring the wrong things, setting targets, paying attention to people rather than the system, understanding failure calls, etc.) will bring the system back into some control and then the data will be much more meaningful and you will see a much closer relationship between what you do and the results.

In summary, start by getting knowledge about individual cases and start collecting data on causes. Experiment with solutions and collect data about what works in order to learn about method. Collect the lagging data to make sure that the changes you are making are having the right impact on your system.

Chapter 5

Principles and practices
for making change happen

The Stoke experience is a good model to follow in order to get started. It is critical to understand that this is not about implementing new procedures and processes but a whole new way of thinking. You are changing from a set of assumptions rooted in mass production thinking to a logic of understanding demand in the context of the citizen and designing against it. If you try and implement new processes without changing the thinking then you will be undermined by the very things you are trying to change.

Existing system	New system
Rational	Normative
Identify problems/crises	What matters – 'good life'
Find solutions, design services	Look for strengths
Implement solutions	Build support and networks – let solutions emerge
Run by and for professionals	Run by citizens who 'pull' for support
'Customer' – consumer of services	Citizen
Purpose: 'be safe', be efficient	Purpose: help build strong citizens and communities

I hope the earlier chapters have illustrated what these statements represent in terms of patterns of assumptions. The one set of alternatives that has not yet been described is 'rational' versus 'normative'. These terms are best described through an example. In the 1960s a group of social scientists in California, Robert Chin, Kenneth Benne and Warren Bennis[1], were tasked with making changes to the state education system. In the process of doing so they took the radical step of researching method as they went. What they found was three methods that characterised the way educational organisations went about the process of change as a process:

- Coercion –'do it or else'.

- Rational – 'this is good for you and here is the evidence, so you should do it too'.

---

1 Chin, R., Benne,K., Bennis. W (1969) *The Planning of Change*. Holt, Reinhart and Winston

- Normative – 'You are very well adapted to the system and I understand that you won't want to change unless you can see for yourself that it makes sense to do so.'

This appears self-explanatory but is quite profound. Clearly, coercion will create change but will not create commitment to change. However, it can be a useful leadership tactic if well managed. For example, a leader might force people to try something different in order to experience a new logic. What needs managing, then, is the learning – someone has to help people understand what the new experience has helped them learn. There are exceptions. Legislation can create change as with seat belts. Once people get used to the practice then cognitive dissonance takes over, 'I see myself complying therefore it must be good for me'. Such outcomes, however, would only be likely to work if the change required is quite simple, i.e. a simple change of activity rather than a change of values or thinking.

Rational change methods are generally ineffective as they primarily polarise people's views. If you already believed in the intended change then having someone tell you that it is good for you is preaching to the converted. If you do not think that way, then being preached to will usually arouse the immune system. If the leader has extraordinary personal credibility then sometimes people choose to change on the basis that 'he or she must right'. Even if this is the case people will often simply adopt new practices without really understanding what they are doing.

In normative change you are trying to change the way people think, not the processes. Chris Argyris[2] calls this 'double-loop learning'. The single loop is the way you currently think, the solution you would adopt without thinking, e.g. the NHS response to the rising demand in A&E is to ask for more resources. The double loop would be to ask why the demand is rising. Similarly, the single loop response to a backlog is to resource a 'backlog busting' effort, whereas the double loop is to ask what is in the backlog and how it got there – prevention.

This is what lies behind the Vanguard method – normative methods around double loop-learning. We are used to using this logic with our clients in the public sector in order to help them change their thinking and therefore their systems. However, the work we and our clients are now doing takes this method to a different level. We have found that we need to help our public sector clients to apply the method to their citizens. Helping clients find out what matters to citizens and communities is to help them carry out normative, double loop learning with citizens. What becomes clear is that you have to help citizens clarify and learn about what really matters to them. In the past help has often been thought of in terms of what others can do for them – they have been told that they have

---

2 http://infed.org/mobi/chris-argyris-theories-of-action-double-loop-learning-and-organizational-learning/

'needs'. The change here is that helping them clarify what matters to them leads to their adopting a perspective that allows them to believe that they can solve their own problems with a bit of help.

The significance is that both providers and receivers have to change. The receivers have to become responsible citizens and the providers have to learn how to encourage and support that change.

Provider	*Citizen & Provider*	*Citizen*
I look for need and provide services.	*The citizen is confident in their own strengths and in the support from experts.*	*I have needs and 'they' provide – it's not my responsibility.*
Existing	Future	Existing

Figure 1. This is a way of characterising the change.

The most helpful process we have found to clarify what matters to citizens is a counselling model developed by Gerard Egan[3]:

- establish trust
- change perspective
- take action.

Trust

To all intents and purposes, you need not worry about doing anything other than establishing trust. Without it you can do nothing. With it, most other things will fall into place (with the proviso that you continue to see your role as asking questions not peddling solutions).

For individuals to trust you they have to feel confident that you know what it is like to be them. That trust is then consolidated when they experience the support as they begin to act. (When trying to gain the trust of a whole community, the tactics and time scale can be different.)

The skills are simple but not easy. Any of the teams will tell you how much difficulty they experienced at first (but only at first – it quickly becomes second nature). It is not enough to ask questions, although that is the core skill. It is important to explore and clarify by saying: 'Tell me more/give me an example/how many/how often.' This helps you and them to fully understand the issues from their perspective. Probably the most important thing to do is to summarise, 'So what you are saying is…'. This consolidates the learning and demonstrates that you have been listening

---

3 Egan, G. (1985) *The Skilled Helper – A Problem–Management Approach to Helping*. Brooks / Cole Publishing Company

and have understood. There are also important things not to do: do not offer opinions, pass comment, offer solutions or interpret what they are saying (i.e. read into the conversation things that were unsaid). The goal is simply to gain clarity on what matters to them and how they currently think about themselves and their status. If you move on too quickly you will hear it in their response, and this must be a signal to you to go back and ask more questions.

The Stoke experience has provided useful insights. There is the beginning of a pattern. The citizen does not necessarily respond just to being helped. What seems to be more significant, in building trust and triggering change, is when they see you provide the same support for someone else. That vicarious experience appears to cement the conviction that this is real for them. What often happens then is that they not only start to help themselves but to help others as well. This is an added bonus as it begins to cement the relationships and networks that are an essential element of communities.

With groups and communities, it is more difficult and time consuming to establish trust. Some examples from the US and described in Green, Moore's and O'Brien's ABCD literature[4] took months or years. You are dealing with established norms in the groups and it may take longer for there to be a consensus about your trustworthiness and the things that matter to the group may be more difficult to action. It is the same behaviour, though, in principle – being there, listening, contributing is what matters. Often it will be a case of fostering individuals who emerge as leaders and working with them to demonstrate your trustworthiness.

Focus is the key. The group will not be a group unless there is something they feel strongly about. Your role is to help them clarify and make concrete that concern without changing it – remember, if they think it's a rat problem, it probably is a rat problem. What you can do is help them create a focus and a place to start. By being aware of the Egan model you can decide whether it needs time to build trust or whether it might be a question of improving the method.

Here's an example closer to home. I referred to the The Beacon and Old Hill estate in Falmouth in Chapter 2. Not only was it run down but it used to be described as a 'no-go' area. I quote from a report by Durie, Wyatt and Stutely:

Overlooking the affluence personified by the gleaming boats in the multi–million pound marina below, the estates had come, by 1995, to

---

4 www.cdf.org.uk/wp–content/uploads/2013/05/An–ABCD–Approach–To–Allocating–Community–First–Funding.pdf

be known to the other communities in Falmouth as 'Beirut'. One of the most deprived areas in Britain, the estate was blighted by violent crime, drug dealing and intimidation.[5]

In 1996, a Bristol University report found that Penwerris, the electoral ward comprising the Beacon and Old Hill estates (having an overall population of 6000, living in 1500 homes), was the most deprived in Cornwall, the county which is, in turn, the most deprived in England. The report also found that it had the largest percentage of children in households with no wage earners, and the second highest number of children living with lone parents. According to the Breadline Britain Index, Penwerris had the highest proportion of poor households of the county's 133 wards. More than 30% of households were living in poverty, well above the national average. Unemployment rates on the estates were 30% above the national average. Of 23 child protection registrations in the council district of Carrick, 19 were for children who lived on the estates. More than 50% of the 1500 homes were without central heating. The illness rate was 18% above the national average.

Not only was the community isolated from the statutory agencies, it was also isolated from and within itself. The common response, when others suffered the effects of crime and vandalism in the community, was one of relief that it had happened to someone else. There was little or no communication, either between the community and the authorities, or amongst the members of the community themselves. Rather, as Bob Mears, the Police Community Liaison and Crime Reduction Officer was later to reflect, there was an attitude among us and other people that everybody who lived on the estate was a criminal. That was obviously not true, but there was no exchange of information.

Hazel Stutely was a health visitor and, after a particularly nasty incident that traumatised a young girl in the estate, Hazel initiated change.There was no plan or strategy. She and her colleagues simply got people and agencies together. Initial meetings, described as 'stormy', demonstrated little apart from a complete lack of trust, so the team selected 20 residents as potential opinion leaders. Five of these agreed to form a working group. As with the US examples, the early focus was on training this group. The team taught them how to apply for grants and awards and how to engage with relevant authorities. The plan, such as it was, emerged from what mattered to the community – identifying the rats, for example. The report describes the key activities that came from the partnership between the estate and the agencies:

---

5 Wyatt KM (2004). CREST: Community Regeneration Evaluating Sustaining and Transferring: Report on the Falmouth Beacon Partnership.

Among the outcomes initially achieved by the partnership was a successful bid led by Penwerris Residents Association for £1.2 million of Capital Challenge funding, matched with a further £1 million funding from Carrick District Council. This money was used to fund central heating and energy efficiency measures, and led to the installation of central heating in 300 properties, with a further 900 properties being re-clad. An old butcher's shop was converted into a Resource Centre, offering training courses and advice on welfare and benefits, as well as being an informal drop-in centre and hub for getting news about the estate. Another disused shop was converted into the Beacon Care Centre, providing a range of healthcare options. This included physiotherapy sessions and health checks for over-65s, alongside confidential nurse-led contraceptive advice and counselling, directly aimed at teenagers on the estate.

The agencies and professional bodies co-evolved with the community. As a consequence, vandalism and crime were no longer seen as other people's problems – rather they were problems confronting the community as a whole.

As trust spread throughout the community, so the community began to be trusted by the authorities, and the community in turn began to trust the agencies.

Over the last seven years, the Beacon Partnership has achieved a series of dramatic health, educational, law and order, and environmental outcomes. Today, a series of initiatives contribute to the ongoing maintenance of the regeneration process. A purpose-built nursery is being constructed, alongside a new youth centre. There are plans for a sensory garden. Money has been secured for landscaping the original Beacon site, from which the estate takes its name. A mosaic project for street names and signs aims to bring the young and elderly to work together with the long-term unemployed of the estate.

Change perspective

The proposition here is, 'if you look at things from this perspective, then better things are possible'. There are two main ways of achieving this. The riskier tactic is to go straight in after you have established a good relationship and ask, 'have you thought about it from this perspective?' For many people this will be a step too far too soon. Some, though, may be able to move faster and may be able to respond. It's a judgement call but it is not irrevocable. If you find that they cannot respond quickly, then carry on building trust until you have evidence that people are ready to think differently.

The less risky option is to build more trust by helping them resolve an immediate and significant problem. The choice of problem is theirs as long as it is 'do-able'. The tactic is that, by removing a barrier that was significant and that they thought was not fixable, you demonstrate your credentials as trustworthy, but also demonstrate what is possible and show that an alternative perspective could work – If we/you did more of this what might it look like?

A key to achieving this in communities, as the example in Falmouth highlights, is the vicarious experience of seeing what is done for others. Some people will be prepared to be pioneers but most want to wait and see before they take part. Often it is a small but symbolic act that makes the difference. In the case of the Beacon and Old Hill estate, one striking example of this was the instance of dog-waste bins. The provision of dog-waste bins on an estate is calculated according to a ratio based on the number of residents in the estate – not the number of dogs. If, as is the case on Beacon and Old Hill, the number of dogs per capita is higher than average, there is a consequent lack of bin provision. On the Beacon and Old Hill estate, the environment was blighted by dog waste. The Partnership worked to deliver more dog-waste bins in order to reflect more accurately the number of dogs on the estate. Within a very short time, dog waste became a problem of the past. In a subsequent survey of tenants and residents that sought to determine the single factor that had the most impact on the estate, a large majority of people identified the provision of adequate numbers of dog-waste bins, and the resultant improvement to the living environment for the community. Here was clear evidence of a dramatic outcome following on from a small intervention, and the momentum this gave to the change process was to lead to a community-wide commitment to the improvement of the environment.

Action

The more skilled we are in establishing trust and changing perspectives the easier it is to move to concrete and effective action. It should be simply, 'If we can do X for you, can you do Y for yourself? And what help will you need to do that?' It's a negotiation – a social contract based on mutual trust.

If it isn't that simple then go back to the beginning and ensure that you have established real trust. Ask some more questions. If you get lost at any stage then return to a core proposition and purpose. Your role is to help citizens build their own strength not to be the expert offering solutions – you ask the questions, they will devise the solutions.

Now all that matters is to ask yourself how you should spend your time as a leader.

Chapter 6

Leadership

It is important to consider who can provide leadership and lead a change in thinking. Logically, the place to start is at the top, with the politicians. But, for all the reasons I've stated in the earlier chapters, this isn't going to work. Vanguard has spent the last ten years trying to get through to them, but the political system is slow to change. Individually, politicians are good enough people but the political system perverts their good intent.

The public sector leaders are now part of that political system and find it difficult to stand up for a different approach. As long as they see their rewards in feeding the beast of Westminster then they too will remain slow to change. This is not to say that we can do nothing. The advent of social media has had a dramatic impact and we should use it to keep up a propaganda battle. Just as ministers' 'good ideas' come from pervading and corridor opinions, we can hijack that process and feed as much of the better logic into it as we can.

The most difficult problem we have to overcome is the perceived method of implementation. There is plenty of evidence that politicians can be wooed by ideas. The Big Society and other initiatives show that they are willing to change but they fail to understand the underlying assumptions that need to change. At present their instinct and practice is to package an idea up, specify outcomes and put it into their commissioning system. This destroys the ideas and also destroys competent organisations who do the work. The government does not yet understand just how incompetent this method of working is. Simply saying, for example, that they will use the voluntary sector to implement ideas is not enough; they must learn how to use these organisations.

The most effective strategy is to demonstrate the alternative method. That means just get on with it! There are increasing numbers of good and competent, local, elected politicians. The election of Police and Crime Commissioners is a good example. Much as the politicians would have liked them to be political enforcers, to toe the party line, they have, in the main, proved to be very independent-minded people bent on doing good work for their areas. This is a great start. If local authorities can learn to work with their elected members as some do (many still see the elected members as the enemy) then a caucus of competence can emerge. Where this happens and where there is good data to support it (viz Stoke) and where local people are vocal in saying that they like what's going on, then it will be very difficult for any politician to stop it.

There are further problems to overcome, however. The government will still not understand the method and logic. Furthermore, an isolated example can remain just that – treated as an exception and ignored as an indicator of what is possible. In his paper for NESTA, Robin Murray[1] talks of new approaches not having sufficient 'capital' yet and that, without it, they remain fringe activities. One way forward is to create local capital and for the pioneers to engage with their neighbouring authorities to create regional examples. The West Midlands is already trying to do this and they will learn how to make it work.

So, for now, the goal is to do as much as we can to demonstrate what is possible. The key is good leadership so I shall first describe what good leadership can and does look like when practised by the people already doing it. The fact that a revitalised front line is learning about what matters from citizens and is acting on that learning to create resilience and independence, does not mean that the role of leader is any less important. Leaders are a resource and they must ask the question, 'What value can I add?'

Let's start by looking at what people need in order to perform well. In a now neglected and out-of-print book, *Motion Study*, Frank Gilbreth outlined these requirements. He showed how to design a system for good performance. I have paraphrased his structure to put it into a more current context:

I will do a good job for you if:

- I know what 'good' looks like, i.e. I have a clear sense of purpose which is shared by everyone around me.
- The organisation is consistent in paying attention to that purpose.
- When my boss turns up he or she is interested primarily in what we are doing that meets purpose and what will help us do more.
- I have data that tells me how well we are meeting purpose and my boss uses that same data to help me meet purpose in better and better ways.
- Everyone around me treats me and my work as important.
- I have the tools, information and training to do the work.
- I am able to make decisions about all the key things I will come across every day.
- I have access to expertise and support when I need it – and it turns up when I need it.

---

[1] Robin Murray. *Danger and Opportunity*. NESTA 2009 www.nesta.org.uk/sites/default/files/danger_and_opportunity.pdf

- My boss helps me work round or solve the pressures that the organisation may create that undermine purpose.

It is the leader's job to ensure these requirements are met.

Purpose

The leader needs to work with everyone to create a clear operational view of 'what we are here for'. By operational I mean a clear statement of what anyone would see if purpose is met. All too often we see anodyne statements of mission, vision or values which are utterly meaningless. I call them corporate wallpaper. You see statements such as the following, for example, about values, 'We will operate at all times with integrity, honesty and a care for citizens'. Who on earth thought you would do anything else?

This is why I prefer the notion of purpose – it is clear and observable and guides behaviour. For example: 'We build strength in communities in order that they can support themselves as much as possible'. A good statement of purpose is constructed through discussion and testing so that those people in your system have ownership and commitment to it. The purpose is then strengthened by deriving a set of principles that guide how purpose will be implemented. This is the importance of the principles that the Stoke team use. Again, it is important that everyone is involved in their derivation but the principles will be around the following logic:

- We seek to find out from citizens what matters to them and act on it.
- We have data measuring our performance against purpose that guides our action and decisions.
- We use the data to find out what works, build knowledge and learn.
- People are responsible for their own work end-to-end (they take ownership and follow it through).
- Expertise is available when needed to support the front line.
- Managers pay attention to the system in order to improve the conditions that support good work and switch off or buffer the conditions that undermine it.

The leader's role is primarily to test purpose and principles. Where and how can this be done? There is only one place to do it and that is 'in the work', with the citizen and with the frontline people. The leader observes what is happening and sees the consequences and effects of what is done. The 'how' is then simple: ask questions about how well what is being done meets purpose and is true to the principles.

Data

I have already said how important data is for creating commitment and enthusiasm. In the new system, data is used to learn and to create feedback for everyone involved. One of your most important questions, therefore, will be 'What does the data tell us?'.

However, before that can be asked, a lot of effort will be needed to derive and test new data. To repeat one of the messages from Chapter 4, the data must be in control charts so that everyone can see what is happening over time. This way everyone can relate action to outcomes. There is nothing more powerful to the front line than seeing a control chart where the data start to rise or fall (whichever is the positive direction) in response to their action, so that they can point to it and say, 'we did that'.

A long–time fan of ours who was determined to act on his enthusiasm is Simon Guilfoyle, who, at the time of writing, is an operational police inspector in the West Midlands. He did not wait for his organisation to change, he simply got on with it. He created a sense of purpose with his teams and encouraged them to use their experience and judgement to do what mattered (he defined this as supporting citizens by reducing crime). He identified what was preventing his officers from spending time on the beat and simply stopped it. For example, they were writing endless reports and constantly asking him for approvals and permissions. None of this was purposeful and so he simply told them it was not necessary and that they could stop doing it. Lest anyone think that no reports were then written, he had discussions with his team about what would constitute purposeful recording, so everyone was committed to doing necessary paperwork but no more than that.

The consequence of this was that crime dropped immediately.

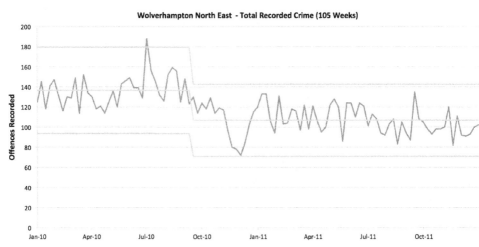

I show you the table above with Simon's permission. When he first showed it to me, the change in performance was so immediate and large that I assumed it was a consequence of redefining what was a crime. "Absolutely not" was his response, "we haven't changed any recording methods. That's genuine reduction in crime." The enthusiasm in his team was palpable. He was ticking all the boxes as a leader but it is hard to understate the power of the data in reinforcing what 'good' looks like – reinforcing clarity of purpose. His team knew that he had the capability to do the right things and get results, and they knew they were in control of doing that and were not simply ciphers in a mindless system.

This is in stark contrast to the countrywide crime data which has shown a steady fall since the mid 1990s. When you mark dates on the graph coinciding with government and police initiatives you can see no discernible change. It is impossible for the police service or the Home Office to say that anything they did made much difference. How much confidence would that give you as a leader to know what to do next? This is the true power of control charts.

For an example of how to take the initiative and make an extraordinary difference I would recommend that you read Simon's book, *Intelligent Policing*[2].

Methods

There are two important principles that underlie the methods that leaders need to adopt:

1. to add value
2. to allow solutions to emerge.

> *a) Frontline teams create value for citizens. The leader's job is to add value to the front line. As leaders spend time with citizens and the front line, seeing what is working, they must seek to find out what gets in the way of purposeful work. In doing this your team will build confidence in you and your ability to make things happen. This in turn will build their confidence in pulling what they need from you at any time, whether it be information, training, support or access to others within and across functions and agencies.*
>
> *b) Starting to work differently does not mean implementing pre-determined solutions however plausible they may seem and even if other agencies have successfully implemented them. You do not have the knowledge that will tell you what works in your own system. The first thing to do is to learn about your system and collect data and knowledge. The successes from other systems can be used to refine the data gathering – test what they have learned and see what is true for*

2 Guilfoyle, Simon (2007) *Intelligent Policing*. Triarchy Press

your system. The only constant, though, is purpose and principles. By being true to them and by applying them you will discover what works and gain confidence in the logic that solutions emerge from the work. This goes against all current practice but is very powerful when you learn to trust it. In the current system, senior managers always want to know when things are going to be implemented and how much savings/improvement it will make. The answer is, 'I don't know but I'll find out'.

The basis of the Vanguard method is that you help people learn, build knowledge and then experiment against data to find better and better ways of making the right things happen.

If we follow the same logic of Purpose, Data and Method then the current system will look something like:

Purpose: *to meet budget, manage resources and implement project plans, i.e do what matters to the hierarchy.*

Data: *to deliver the right management numbers, costs and targeted performance – pay attention to significant variance.*

Method: *implement solutions, carry out appraisals and implement follow-up training plans; act on problems.*

It couldn't be more different from the system you will seeking to create. The good news is that, as Simon Guilfoyle has shown, it is not overly difficult to manage.

If you pay attention to what matters to citizens, and you have data that shows what has been done and how effective it has been, then you will have more and better information and knowledge than anyone else in the organisation. That knowledge is power is indisputable. Your management data in the traditional format will also go in the right direction – costs will go down and performance will go up. There may be some issues, as in the care organisation in Chapter 2 whereby you learn that spending more 'here' will save lots 'there', where 'there' is in someone else's department or agency. In practice, therefore, there may be difficulties in negotiating across boundaries but you do have the data so you are as well armed as anyone could be.

Even when purpose has been defined, knowledge learned, data tested and frontline teams are working confidently, there is still important work to do. As the front line learns how to listen and act it seems as though the job has been done. It is such a revelation to people and there is always the sense that they're over the hurdle. The reality is that the leadership job has not even begun. The work that people are doing is the direct opposite of the way the system has been working historically. Everything in that system will undermine and block what they are trying to do. The leader's role is crucial and tackles these problems. Some things may be simple but in many cases the leader will need to find a way to work round the existing system. At the same time you can try to engage other departments with data and stories from the new work in order to encourage them to be helpful. The real work, however, is to make the changes systematic and permanent so that the organisation actively supports the new design. That will take time and skill.

So, for example, a common problem is that the current system is based on hierarchies of grades and qualifications. You quickly learn that this is not only irrelevant but unhelpful. What happens is that the front line is happy to ignore this for a while but when you have to redeploy people, employ new people or change structures and acknowledge different skills, the HR system rapidly becomes a blockage. A strong leader acknowledges this problem and then seeks to change it.

The problems are, at least, obvious. The leader does not have to plan for them. It is best done empirically – as the teams start doing the right things, any problems will emerge, and leaders then have the confidence that they are tackling the right problems and can see the needed outcome. For example, a common problem in children's services is the so-called transition where they move through age-defined barriers. There is a service that covers their need until they reach a particular age and then they are handed over, not simply to another scheme, but usually to another organisation.

One example of the effects of this is that of Tracey (not her real name) who was due to leave school. She had strong autistic spectrum conditions. A new location was found for her which, on the face of it, would cater for her. In the current system this is considered to be a totally new provision with new funding and new conditions. What matters most to autistic people is continuity and trusting relationships. The 'transition', by necessity, means that everything has to change. But Tracey had not changed.

The result was a predictable and self-fulfilling stupidity. Tracey's behaviour became very problematic for the new institution and within four weeks she had been excluded. The cost grew, both financially and in terms of the strain on Tracey and her family. What was needed was for the support worker, with whom Tracey had a strong relationship, to follow her through the transition but budgets and structures would not allow this. A good leader could have resolved this problem.

In another example a social care team was following the principles in exemplary fashion. They had set aside their role as 'professional' social workers and simply behaved as concerned individuals, worked across teams and finding very creative ways of brokering support in the community. Their work is now less and less provision of services and more and more making it possible for people to help themselves and each other. The one thing they often have to provide, however, is transport. The transport is managed across several budget holders. There is a fleet manager for staff vehicles, taxi budgets for special educational needs transport and at least two other functional teams with responsibility for transport requirements. This has made it quite problematic for the frontline teams to supply transport easily when needed. They are doing it but not in a sustainable way nor in the cheapest way. This, again, needs a good leader to sort it out.

I came across a good example of how strong leadership had solved a problem that bedevils all public sector organisations. A standard feature of the design of many processes is assessment and referral. In social services every new contact needs to be assessed to see if they are eligible. In policing, it is not called assessment but frontline officers attend, assess, record and pass on work to other teams. Assessment and referral is pointless and serves only to defer or avoid providing any help. Even when frontline teams make this connection (as they do very quickly) it is usually viewed by managers as an intractable problem needing unaffordable and unrealistic changes to the IT systems and regulatory frameworks.

Monmouth Social Services, however, simply decided to change it. They first adopted a new principle, which was to make any recording purposeful. In other words, only information needed to help the citizen and/or help the system learn was to be collected. They involved the IT team from the start and within a surprisingly short time they had devised a very simple front-end recording system that was very easy to use and from which the essential information could be viewed, aggregated and fed into whatever other system needed it.

The real obstacles to changing thinking are rarely technical problems but problems of political will, i.e. leadership. The power of solving this problem is to demonstrate that other problems can be tackled if there is the will to do it. The problems may not be easy or simple but the will to tackle them is the vital component.

There is a very important rider to the activity of a good leader. It is not enough to make the changes and tackle the problems. The leader must always go back to the front line and ensure that their efforts have paid off and that the system is indeed working better as a consequence. This not only builds the leader's confidence but also that of the front line. Historically, frontlines hate it when leaders turn up. It usually indicates that something has gone wrong. The test of a good leader is that frontline teams always want them to turn up because they know that the leader is only interested in making things work better for them.

Tackling the wider system across organisations is even more challenging but also indicative of the cost in time and effort that will be needed in order both to make life easier for people and to see the true economic return from this thinking. An example of this can be shown through the case of Charlie, who was also autistic. He was described as pleasant but difficult. When he was 16 he was attacked by someone living with him. He defended himself and severely injured his attacker. Had he not been autistic he would have ended up in prison. As it was he spent the next 20 years in a Special Hospital. Those close to him were keen to get him out. It was important that he was released without condition and out of the review system that would otherwise continue to plague him and those round him.

It took a huge amount of time and effort but Charlie is now living independently with the support of a good friend. Had this not happened the best the system would have done would have been to simply release him into some alternative special service. No one would have challenged what they thought they knew about him. That might have salved some consciences but it would have been very expensive and would have done Charlie little good. As it is he costs the state very little and he is thriving.

I have been careful not to identify who leaders need to be. Clearly the more positional power you have (the further up the hierarchy you sit) the more influence you have within your remit to make changes, but what we have found is that it is often the people close to the front line who 'get it' first. Simon Guilfoyle is a good example – he was a sergeant when he first started transforming policing.

You can lead from a position as first among equals – it's not what's on the organisation chart that makes the difference, it's what is in your head. Anyone can be a good leader. The key is to look at the system from the citizen's perspective, see what matters and help the front line to make it work. Purposefully.

Chapter 7

The Economic case

The economics of this new approach to public services is unequivocal and compelling. We know that the current system is not only unsustainable but self-defeating – we spend more and more money and create more and more failure.

It is obvious that the more you do for someone, the less they will do for themselves. The more you treat citizens as consumers, the less responsibility they will take for themselves. The more you disenfranchise the personal networks with 'keep safe' procedures, the less people can do for each other and the more isolated people become. At the very least, it would be helpful if politicians and public sector leaders could recognise this and admit that they do not know what else to do.

Part of the problem is that politicians are short-term thinkers – they want to be seen to achieve a lot in the short time they are in power. Longer-term strategies have no immediate political capital, so, for example, while we have known about the failure to rehabilitate prisoners for a very long time, all that ever happens is that funding is cut back time and time again. Cost matters to politicians as it does to us, which is why it is imperative for us to show them how to change the system – we can never rely on them to 'get it'. They have shown no sign of doing so in my lifetime.

Here is an example to show the criminal stupidity of how money is spent without sufficient accountability

James is autistic and went undiagnosed until he was a teenager. He had been bullied relentlessly, had become an elective mute and was self-harming. His local authority placed him with a specialist home, which happened to be at the other end of the country. His parents moved to be close to him. His £130,000 annual cost of containment, for that's what it was, continued to be paid and was so for 11 years. Being so far away from the original local authority there was never any thought of reviewing the case – they just kept paying. It was only when his original social worker retired and wanted to tidy up his case work that a review was triggered.

By this time, James had become a very annoyed and frustrated person. When asked, as part of the review, what a good life would look like, he said, "I want to pay tax". In other words he wanted to be a contributor and, to him, a worthwhile human being. He wanted to go to college. It took a lot of time and effort to get him out of the home but he went to college. He needed support because he became stressed easily and found that difficult to manage. He still does but he is now a director of an advocacy organisation and has a good friend who acts as his stress manager when needed. James now costs the state nothing but it will take some time yet for the system to work for people like James and some time, therefore, before the true costs are taken out of that system.

As a leader you will need to confront the economics. There will be an immediate challenge about affordability so it helps if you are prepared to show a case that places doubt on the affordability of the current system as well as the affordability of the new system. The leaders we have worked with need time to understand the full implications of this approach and will always ask, 'where's the money coming from, where are the savings'.

The economic case builds up in layers. An important consideration throughout is the distinction between fixed and variable costs. Variable costs – the costs you can save by not doing something – are easy to act on, but fixed costs are more difficult. You still have to pay your staffing and office costs even if you choose not to do things. However, the essence of the economic argument is to focus on 'value' rather than 'cost'. Value can be defined as what matters to the citizen. If the system concentrates on doing exactly and only what matters to the citizen, then costs will come down automatically. This sounds obvious but accepting that costs go down by helping citizens directly will require a huge shift in thinking. The Utah example of housing the homeless shows how counter intuitive it is to consider value before cost.

The lever for reducing cost is doing what matters at the first point of contact. In most organisations this has an immediate effect. By contrast, most of the existing systems have designed their front ends to 'classify, label and process' the contact in order for it to be passed to the so-called 'back office' for assessment and further referral. In anyone else's language this is a 'make work' system. It arises because productivity-driven managers believe it protects their higher paid experts. In reality it swamps everyone with rubbish and waste. Not only does the work tend to be redone in the current system but it is usually not re-done efficiently and creates duplication, mistakes and rework of work that did not need doing in the first place. The reduced cost of doing it just the once, without all the rework is clear:

A police force simply gave its frontline officers the freedom to use their experience, training and initiative (why wouldn't you?) to do what mattered to the caller or whatever was merited in the circumstances. At the time they were running a monthly task list (all the jobs that had accumulated for officers to do) of 1200 items in one station alone. As soon as officers started resolving issues at point of contact instead of feeding them into the system, the task list evaporated to just 17 after one month of the new regime. Think of the work no longer being done: officers not having to revisit jobs, admin staff not having to process task lists, supervisors not having to compile lists, allocate work, chase work, account for work, etc. Officers quickly reported having more time available and then the Police Constable Support Officers (PCSOs) reported having nothing to do. The senior officers had not realised that such was the work load created by the system of creating task lists that the PCSOs had been informally drafted in to help out. Over time this had become their full time job rather than the neighbourhood work for which they had been recruited.

In one month, another larger force found that by resolving non-emergency issues at first point of contact they created the equivalent of 62 officer's capacity.

In the short term, it is much more helpful to view the time freed up as 'capacity' rather than cost. Even if you classified it as cost, you probably couldn't realise the benefits very quickly – this is the fixed cost problem. In any case the capacity is more important to the system at this stage as it creates time and resource to help with experimentation and learning. There will be plenty of things that there has not been the capacity to do that are of value to citizens and the system will need to learn how to do them – spare capacity will not go amiss.

This early phase allows the organisation to learn the true value of its people and the functions and what they are currently doing as opposed to what would be purposeful. As the front line becomes more competent and capable and learns how to do what matters you learn what capability needs to be pulled. This may be to augment the capability, or to carry out specific tasks where the skills are missing. What had been a plethora of functional teams becomes a 'cupboard' of resources. It will become obvious what is and is not needed. A less obvious benefit is that the experts now do what they do with the front line and so those frontline teams learn capability from the experts and are able to do more and more themselves.

This leads to a second tier of cost saving opportunities. The police force in the last example had many centralised functions. As in most organisations, these functions created their own demand in order to justify the targets they were expected to meet. As soon as the front line started resolving issues instead of feeding them into the system for labelling and processing, much of the central work withered on the vine.

An example of such a function came about through Home Office concerns about police not taking action on incidents concerning people who were being victimised in their communities. This led to police forces creating 'vulnerable people' teams. The reality was that 'vulnerable people' received more attention but no action – the work was to create records to prove to HMIC that 'the force was paying attention'. This was not a cynical as it sounds – it is the normal way things work to keep the regulator happy. When the new system was introduced, the frontline officers simply took responsibility for the incidents and genuinely helped people. The vulnerable people team had no work to do except keep their records.

The leaders were now able to view work from the perspective of what was 'purposeful' and to ask why anything not 'purposeful' was being maintained. This led to a period of readjustment that was quite subtle and gradual. After twelve months, and without losing any police officers, they had saved £12m. The probability is that they could not tell you how they had done it. It came from simply seeing the organisation from the citizen backwards, seeing what was 'purposeful' from that perspective and losing what was not purposeful.

A neighbouring police force reported a £14m savings in a year. Both would say that they had changed perspective but had barely started in terms of the fundamental changes they wanted to make. Even so, contrast these results with the usual negligible results from other methods, such as process improvement.

The savings from reconciling specialist functions are twofold. First, you need fewer functions and secondly, work that was considered 'expert' and essential turns out not to be necessary. Being a good listener appears to be the prime requirement. There is thus less need for expensive specialist training programmes, higher pay for alleged expertise, separate managers for professional departments and more. Even without knowledge of the skills actually needed, managers will find it useful to ask what purpose any training currently carried out actually serves.

At this time, neither force had approached the third tier of opportunity, and that is to structure the force to meet purpose. Once frontline capability has been established and the logic of purpose has become clear then the overall functional structure of the organisation comes into focus – how does the way we are structured support purpose? In the existing system work has been broken down into simple activities and functionalised. Each function not only has its management structure but becomes a self-fulfilling entity intent on its own survival rather than the greater good. Functions compete for resources and have long since forgotten how to cooperate. In the existing system real cooperation is seen as a senior management requirement to be imposed but this simply does not happen – functionalised budgets maintain rather than diminish the separation. Most of the money is consumed in managing the functions rather than delivering any competent output. Radical simplification and reduction both in layers and in spread of function must be a major opportunity for savings.

In the early stages of change, there is still the cost of having to manipulate the wider system that is not yet congruent with the new way of doing things. This is time spent producing data for the old system, continuing with useless projects and attending meetings that only serve the hierarchy.

The teams in Stoke and Bromsgrove wanted to understand both the cost and activity relationship in terms of both pre intervention and post intervention activity. The approach the team adopted was to identify all the activity that had been carried out with an individual for a two-year period prior to working with them in the new way. This required collecting the data across all the partner agencies who had worked with citizens over that two-year window. The two year period was selected as it was felt to give a representative picture of activity over a reasonable time frame. This data would then be compared with activity that had been carried out with the citizens post intervention.

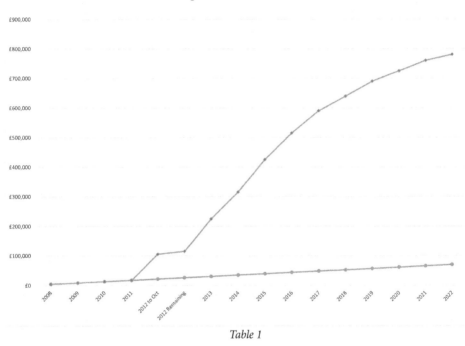

Table 1

Table 1 shows the data for a typical case in Bromsgrove. The council team intervened in 2011. The annual costs since then have been close to £70,000. Had they not intervened, a very conservative estimate shows the costs rising to £700,000. And had they not intervened, four children would have been taken into care. The graph shows the costs of that care. It does not show what might have happened as a consequence – the lifetime problems of children who go into care are well documented and represent a huge cost on society. This is yet another problem that a focus on cost prevents us from tackling.

When you look at the data for the first seven cases in Stoke, aggregated together, the following picture emerges:

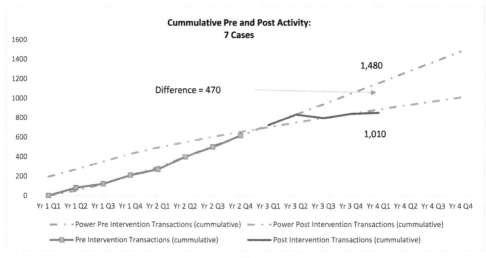

Table 2

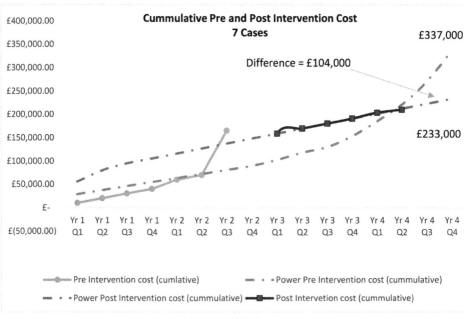

Table 3

Table 2 shows the number of transactions across all agencies and Table 3 shows the cost. The tables simply show what was achieved while the team was learning how to intervene. Much more will be achieved as the team improves its methods and knowledge?

The full quantity of these savings can never be predicted but will always be significant: switch off waste and failure demand, act on demand rather than feed it into the system, subordinate functions to demand (pull) and then decide how much purposeful management you need. The bigger savings are yet to be realised because the simple fact is that public sector agencies are not citizen-shaped.

If you design something that is citizen-shaped there is a near certainty that it will cross agency boundaries. The Stoke team found this immediately. Most profiles of what mattered to the citizens involved housing, health, education and criminal justice. They costed each case as they went along, in terms of both what the case had cost so far, and what the costs would have been to all agencies had they not intervened. Here is a typical example:

Cost Analysis Comparison

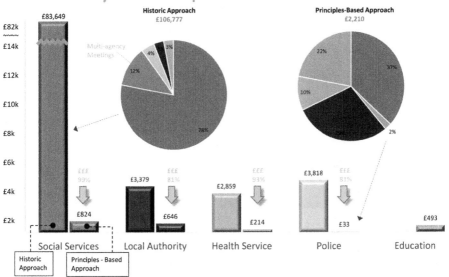

Pre-intervention costs and projecting those forwards for another two years, would mean that each person cost the wider system over £337,000 per year. The average cost post-intervention was predicted to be £233,000. This figure was obtained by taking the pre-intervention costs up to the point of intervention, then adding the post-intervention costs and projecting these forward two years to give a cost comparison. It is accepted that the figures lack real statistical validity because the sample size is so small but they do give a flavour of what might be possible.

The following table shows how costs have shifted across agencies in Stoke for the 7 cases identified above.

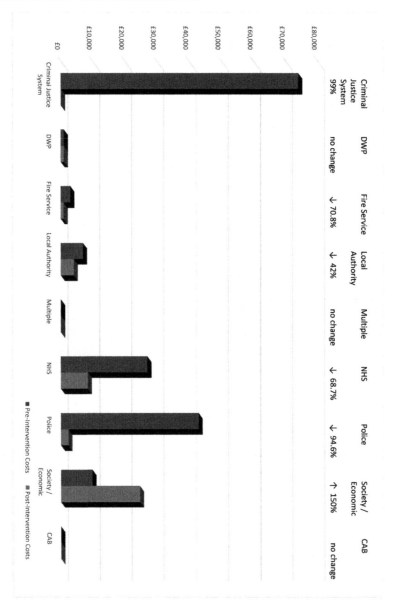

The table shows that costs have fallen for almost every agency in the system, with the Criminal Justice system the biggest winner. It no longer has to pursue citizens through the legal system with its expensive court and legal fees.

The team created a box on the chart called Society and Economics. This was the only box which showed an increase in costs. These costs included, for example, those for the increase in alcohol and drug rehabilitation services that were required to help citizens. The old world system restricts the amount of these types of services that it buys on the basis of the money that it has available. What is clear from the work being done in Stoke is that there is plenty of resource (money and people) in the current system but that it may need to be reapportioned across the system in order to make the sustainable individual savings of £14,857 per person identified above. To take this forward will require a change in thinking away from functionally specialist organisation designs to one that considers and works across organisations for the good of the whole system. In other words, it shows the waste, cost and futility of current public sector design.

Another key question that needs answering is how many citizens are out there that we need to work with? In Stoke the team developed the targeting system shown in Chapter 1. It shows the small number of households and people that create the current demand. The cost of helping these people has already been shown to be a third lower.

Imagine if the public sector were citizen shaped and developed the knowledge to be able to not only target the right people but through that learning prevent problems occurring. In Chapter 4, I mentioned the work of Greater Manchester Police in identifying domestic violence as a clear cause of major criminality. What other problems will be switched off by acting on these causes?

The voluntary sector represents yet another tier of economic opportunity. Suppose we take the same logic to the voluntary sector as we do to the public sector. Each voluntary organisation now has to survive by building an administration, bidding for funds, marketing itself, attracting volunteers and promoting its success. This consumes enormous collective resource and in the current system is particularly onerous. Only the larger charities can afford the means to bid and the annualised grants mean constant lack of security for employees, and thus constant turnover. The overlap between voluntary organisations is growing. I am struck by two apparent phenomena. First, the vast sums of money that they manage collectively combined with the vast apparent unmet need in society. Secondly, the sheer proliferation. In my own small locality, which is a sparse rural area, there are 800 plus voluntary organisations. Yet, each does the same thing in principle – they seek to rebuild peoples' strengths and help them to be resilient and independent. The charities, however, suffer the same problems as the public sector. They 'hunt the need', they promote their role as experts and they deal with 'bits' of people rather than the people in context. *De facto*, the same rampant functionalism has evolved in the third sector as has evolved in public agencies. The best ones do the right things but the existing system of commissioning and regulation is making this more and more difficult for them. I was involved with a programme run by Barnardos some years ago. They were rehabilitating young offenders in Edinburgh. They had learned that the process required initial mentoring by Barnardos people but success was only achieved by building links within their communities and establishing community based mentors. Barnardos had learned that this process took at least eighteen months and yet the contract to do the work as supplied by the local authority was for 11 months.

I live in a small rural community and a lot of the people I know are volunteers for some charity or other. Most travel for that work. Just suppose that all those people became a community asset instead, where they were organised to help anyone in their own community. This could be achieved very easily as an extension of the Local Area Coordination philosophy and practices described in Chapter 2. There might be a need for expertise and research but this would evolve empirically as would the best means for supplying it. My guess would be that the total pot of money required to run such a system would be a fraction of that currently donated. Furthermore, the coffers of the state would have more capability to meet such requirements without the phenomenal current waste.

The macro economics

Tim Jackson, in his book, *Prosperity Without Growth*[1] makes a powerful case for an alternative economic structure. The current system is addicted to 'growth' and he argues compellingly that this is also self-defeating. It is based on a constant encouragement for citizens to be consumers. What is particularly relevant to this book is the effect on the citizen of being a consumer. We buy stuff for more than utilitarian purposes. The stuff we buy says who we are, bolsters our self-worth and positions us in our society – it has deep significance. Yet, at the same time, it corrodes our very wellbeing. The data are clear. In the most liberal of market economies (the USA and UK) the health and wellbeing indicators are the lowest in the developed world. In the managed market economies (Germany, Scandinavia *et al.*) they are slightly better. One of the main correlates with poor wellbeing is inequality of earnings. Jackson suggests that two changes are needed: first, governments need to change what they measure to reflect both finite resources on our planet and the harm to society of consumerism. Secondly, we need to change the citizens' addiction to the social trappings of consumerism. This latter is obviously a complex task. However, the more we can rebuild communities, the more value

---

1 Jackson, T (2011) *Prosperity without Growth* ,Routledge

people will derive from their involvement in them. It will be a good test of Jackson's task – how much could it start to wean us off consumerism by default?

Overall, then, the economic case is compelling. In order to make it work much has to change. The mechanics, including how to structure and budget for local services, would seem to be difficult enough but appear straightforward compared to the intransigent and inappropriate assumptions in the existing administrations. The task is to create more and more examples and build Robin Murray's capital.

PART TWO

The Logic of the Current System

Chapter 8

Getting things done
in the current system

Politicians want to make their mark. They have campaigned on a manifesto and they want to implement it. But the desire to get things done immediately puts the politician into potential conflict with the public sector.

The politicians have two sets of problems – influencing the departmental civil servants through whom they have to implement their ideas, and influencing the professionals, the teachers, doctors and police officers, etc. who have to engage with the ideas. The generous view is that politicians would like to be able to trust frontline public professionals but the experience and 'folklore' around the Derek Hattons of this world make them worry – 'we simply can't trust them even though we'd love to'. The less generous view is that there is an established prejudice against the motives of civil servants and a belief that public sector workers are intransigent and self-interested.

Either way, Her Majesty's Government (HMG) tends to get things done by prescribing the results and testing against the prescription. This is the basis of the 'targets' culture. It was during the New Labour years that targets were established and they have remained *de facto*. Politicians haven't done enough research into how else to get things done and underestimate the degree to which targets have been encoded in an organisation's DNA. If anyone thinks targets are a thing of the past then they should see the frontlines of public sector organisations for themselves. Targets are alive and well, as I shall discuss later in this chapter.

Targets

It is important to clarify the semantics. Everyone would agree that aspirational targets are sensible: to improve National Health Service outcomes, to ensure more students have a better education, etc. A problem arises when numerical targets are used to manage the system on a daily basis. It is this management by targets that is the problem. Many politicians recognise this but when it comes to doing something about it they reluctantly acknowledge that they know of no alternative. They use language like: 'Maybe we can have fewer/better targets.'

Inevitably, there are political reasons for the selection of targets. In many cases I believe they are chosen to reflect what politicians think matters but in others it is simply to get votes. Either way, there are two fundamental pieces of information missing – evidence and knowledge: evidence as to what matters and why to the general public, and knowledge of what is and is not working and why. In the absence of understanding the problem to be solved, the presumed causes are tackled out of context. There is even less understanding involved in choosing the particular numbers that become the targets to be managed. For example, the introduction of the A&E waiting time target was entirely plausible but there was little, if any, consideration as to why waiting times were a problem. Some NHS professionals knew that many people attended A&E unnecessarily but they didn't know why or what for. The hospitals were required to impose the target while still coping with an extra work load. The wider system set up walk-in centres, NHS Direct and minor injury units with no evidence that they were solving the right problems. 'Here's the solution – now what was the problem?'

In my many conversations over the years about targets I have noticed an incredulity amongst those in Westminster. It expresses itself as 'surely intelligent managers and frontline staff should see targets for what they are and still seek to do what they know is right'. This is very worthy but it fails to understand the full nature of the system of targets. If it were simply an order from on high then I think most people would indeed find ways round it and continue to do the right thing. I remember one of my first consultancy jobs was with a subsidiary of a foreign firm. Every month HQ demanded management data; it was seen as a nuisance, deflecting time and effort and had little relevance to the operation in the UK. So, the finance director decided to send a set of made-up numbers that varied up to five per cent from the previous month so it looked plausible, and he was never found out. It was an entirely sensible response. However, the public sector does not have such an opportunity. The targets are rigorously inspected. Each sector has its inspectorate who can be counted on to be intrusive and thorough in what they do. On the face of it they are there to ensure that the agency they inspect is doing good things but what they inspect is pre-determined and built around the targets. This sets the target culture in stone.

Whatever ministers say to the contrary, 'you get what you inspect'. Inspection also encompasses the 'citizen safety' problem. Following scandals and enquiries, a raft of new procedures will be issued and the inspection system will ensure compliance. The role of the public servant is to comply.

The system is full of contradictions based on the can we/can't we trust 'them' dilemma. The outcome of any inquiry is a whole new set of training requirements – 'train them and they'll do it'. The paradox is this: why do we trust people less and less and specify what they should do and, at the same time, increase their training and impose ever more rigorous appraisal. This apparent paradox was recognised by Max Weber who developed his views of bureaucracies. His 'ideal' bureaucracy consisted of six central elements:

1. Clearly defined division of labour.
2. Hierarchical structures of offices.
3. Written guidelines prescribing performance criteria.
4. Recruitment to offices based on specialisation and expertise.
5. Office-holding as a career or vocation.
6. Duties and authority attached to positions not persons.

I quote Weber because I believe it is one of the best ways to describe the bureaucratisation of the public sector. There is this overwhelming sense that you are dealing with a mindless system and that the individuals you meet would love to help you but are bound to do what their role prescribes. I had a biopsy procedure recently and the young doctor read a whole set of stuff to me about what might go wrong. I blanched so comprehensively that they had to stop until I recovered. The procedure was simple and might even have taken less time than her introduction. I said to her, "Why did you have to scare the stuffing out me, why couldn't you have just got on with it?" "Ah, those were the days", she said. It was more important to comply with the concerns of the system than to provide a sensible briefing relevant to any concerns I may have had.

Weber was writing a hundred years ago and it is important to ask why it is still not only the prevailing model but one that administrations return to and amplify.

Specification and inspection

A government (or any management structure) believes it can achieve goals by specifying what people are to do – tell them, write it down and they'll do it. In the private manufacturing sector this is done by 'numbers' – the targets that specify what needs to be sold, produced, processed, etc. This is also the case in the public sector. Government is well-intentioned in clarifying what it thinks matters to citizens and believes that the targets it sets are improving general outcomes. So, what's wrong with that? For example, government believes, rightly, that citizens want to be seen quickly by doctors and sets waiting targets for GPs and hospitals. If patients are seen more quickly that can only be good – can't it? Unfortunately not. Good doctors who want to be thorough and do the right thing put themselves under potentially unsustainable pressure. What are they supposed to do? Some cope by limiting what they do per visit and others solve the problem by referring patients to consultants more quickly than they might otherwise have done. In A&E a member of staff is often employed to 'see' the patient and establish basic facts but without any medical intervention. This qualifies as 'seeing' the patient but achieves nothing but additional cost to the system.

Much has been written about how these targets distort behaviour. It is not the targets themselves but the way managers use them. In the public sector, government pays attention to the targeted performance as an indicator of the competence of the agency and rewards and punishes accordingly. It is no surprise, therefore, that public sector leaders see it as their *de facto* purpose to meet the targets. Public vilification and sackings were not unusual at the height of the Blair government's performance management regime. And what, would you suppose, in such a culture were those public sector leaders paying attention to in their own organisations? It is this culture that is the problem – how the measurement of the targets drives what is seen to matter. And in this respect it is little different in the public and private sectors.

How the target culture works

The classic problem of the target mentality is that you get what you count, not what counts. The limits to this way of thinking are so obvious that it begs the question as to why people cannot see it. For instance, waiting times to see GPs can be counted and a target imposed, but this will tell you nothing about the quality of care for the patient – the actual purpose of seeing a GP. The problem for government, I believe, is the frustration of wanting to see some outcomes but not knowing how to achieve this without the imposition of targets.

There is a difference between public and private sectors and that is in the purpose of the targets. In the private sector, they are purely numbers-driven (to keep analysts happy). There is often a deception involved in that they have to sanitise them so 'sales' targets are dressed up as good customer service; call handling targets likewise. At least in the public sector the targets were and are set with the intention of benefitting the citizen. However, within the public sector hierarchy, the only daily reality is 'make the numbers'. Whilst government and, in my experience, departmental civil servants believe that everyone is improving the system, the frontline organisation is simply improving the numbers. In reality, what else would you expect them to do?

It is hard to believe that politicians fail to understand what is happening. I heard a story about Tony Blair attending an education conference and on being told by a head teacher that schools were excluding 'no hope' pupils in order to maximise the GCSE grades, he was clearly shocked; just as he was when challenged on an election tour about similar behaviour in the NHS. He couldn't believe such behaviour was possible. I spoke to an Audit Commission manager at that time and she was similarly aghast at the lengths people were going to in order to meet targets. Her quote will stay with me: "That really wasn't what we intended."

Unintended consequences are one thing – systemic inability to understand them is another. For example, the Welsh Assembly took a bold and welcome step of making shops charge for carrier bags. Only later did it transpire that while the use of carrier bags had dropped by 80%, use of bin liners had risen dramatically. Needless to say, bin liners are more expensive to produce and less environmentally friendly than supermarket bags. So, some consequences can be quite subtle but politicians seem unable to anticipate or spot the more obvious ones. Or they spot them and choose to ignore inconvenient outcomes.

Stories from the era of Blair's target regime keep recurring. The Accident and Emergency (A&E) target is not the only one still operating. The eighteen-week treatment target is still alive and well – more than can be said for some of the patients! – and is still subject to much manipulation. There are many common dodges and consequences. For example, if the eighteen weeks have passed – known as a breach – then there is little incentive for you to be seen. Also, targets are achieved more easily by seeing patients with simple problems. People are treated according to the likelihood of them breaching the target rather than because of their need. The system also encourages cheating the numbers. If you are offered an appointment and can't make it, the clock is reset and the eighteen weeks start all over again. There is a parallel target for 'long waits' and NHS trusts have a constant problem of juggling the two. One trust I know of would drip feed the long waits into the schedule to try and balance both targets. Once again, patients are not being seen according to clinical need but according to target manipulation. You can sense the politicians' anxiety. They know it's wrong but they know no other method.

Targets also have more subtle and complex consequences. Target logic infects the whole system so that people get used to it and fail to see it for what it is. A good example is the planning system in local authorities. The prime responsibility of the planners is to designate the use of land and ensure that good quality and effective development is allowed and the converse refused. They have to operate within government priorities and manage any resultant conflicts.

Government decided that the planners were holding up commercial enterprise and that citizens were unhappy with what was seen as unnecessary delays in dealing with applications. Government was, reasonably, concerned that applicants, whether commercial or private, should be able to progress their schemes with minimal delay. They introduced a target that domestic plans should receive a response within eight weeks and larger plans (invariably commercial) within thirteen weeks (very large schemes had their own guidance).

The planners achieved a default position very quickly. With no particular cynicism they learned that the easiest way reach the target was to say 'no'. Thus refusal rates rose from around 2% to 30% within a couple of years. When the inspectors noticed this, the planners learned to call applicants and ask them to withdraw any application they were about to refuse. The target simply engaged their ingenuity. This wasn't noticed because it wasn't measured. What mattered to the applicant was how long it took for the planners to say 'yes' but that wasn't being measured either. And, of course, for many applicants a positive decision was now taking longer and longer. There was no limit to the number of times the planners could refuse an application. Architects and agents quickly learned to allow a couple of years for anything remotely complicated.

Internally many changes were taking place. Each department needed to be clear when the eight-week clock started. This also needed to be agreed with the inspectors. The clock would start when the applicant had supplied everything and when everything supplied complied with the planners' standards of presentation. They called this a 'valid' application.

Teams were set up in each department whose job it was to validate applications, i.e. take them through the process of as much 'to-ing and fro-ing' as was necessary to reach the arbitrary standard of 'valid'. Whereas applications had historically been seen by the planners on day one it was now often weeks before they had sight of them. When they did, they usually found problems that the validation team hadn't spotted but then had the pressure of resolving them after the clock had started ticking. The longer the process took, the more calls came in, adding to the pressure on resources. It became a common complaint from agents that they could never get hold of anyone for a sensible conversation. This had the unfortunate consequence of portraying the planners as uninterested and obstructive.

I came across an example where a planning department had brought in a very expensive manufacturing consultancy in order to improve its processes. The consultants had spotted the 'time from receipt to planners' desk' problem and decided to solve it. In six months they reduced the times by around half. No-one, least of all the planners, had spotted that the problem had only existed as a result of the target, i.e. the creation of an admin team to validate the plans in order to decide when the clock started.

Perhaps more insidious was the fact that the pressures of meeting the target and being seen to meet the target (being seen as 'upper quartile', i.e. in the top 25% of planning departments) meant that the purpose of having planners was largely ignored – they simply did not have time to do it. They had all had years of experience and training in order to understand the use, value and economics of land and buildings. They valued the notion of good design and judgement yet they had been reduced largely to mere processors of planning applications. Design had become a forgotten concept and pre-application advice became something that they charged for as opposed to being their core purpose. The system was so bad that applicants were happy to pay for it – at least they then actually saw a planner.

The psychology of targets is perverse. Everyone hates them and yet it is so easy to develop a need for them. If the target is removed managers lose feedback – and performing 'well' means avoiding attention and censure. For example, the police service has a core target around detection rates. One of its main jobs, of course, is to catch criminals. Yet, when chief officers in two forces realised that paying attention to detection rates was causing officers to do the wrong things and removed the emphasis on the target, there was considerable discomfort at the front line. There were two responses: most said, 'so what are you going to measure, because we need to know what you want from us?' and others actually concluded that, 'we don't have to arrest people any more'. Such is the perversity that is built in, and on which the system becomes dependent.

Specification of method – not just 'the what' but 'the how'.

The target principle has been extended far beyond the primary outcomes envisaged. In many parts of the public sector, HMG has decided that it needs to specify not just what is achieved but how it is achieved. The result is that particular processes have been defined, with their own targets. The drivers for this level of specification are varied: some, like child protection, are the outcome of reviews or enquiries following high profile cases. Right across the social services sector, for example, targets and procedures stress 'time to assess' to the point that it is tempting to observe that the purpose of social services is just to assess. The logic is plausible in that it enforces 'fairness', so that everyone receives the same level of support and access. And you can see the dilemma. It is so plausible. How could anyone argue with the enforcement of assessment – 'of course they need to be assessed, we need to understand what people need'. The truth is somewhat different, of course. Assessment leads to consideration of level of need which in turn leads to a decision as to whether they are eligible for services. Assessment is more to do with gate-keeping than service. Furthermore, assessment puts labels on people and describes how well they fit a service rather than what matters to them, so the service they get may be of little value anyway.

Policing has also been subjected to detailed specification of method. For example, when the government responded to a public survey about 'fear of crime' they set about directing the police to address it. That same survey revealed to the Home Office that fear of burglary and robbery (street muggings) were the top two concerns. This was then added to by legislation that enshrined the notion that the victim's view of crime was paramount, in other words, if the victim believed a crime had been committed against them, and they were indeed a 'victim', then a crime had been committed. David Blunkett, the then Home Secretary, wanted to make what he thought was a clear statement to the law-abiding citizen – that the politicians were listening to their fears and concerns.

The police had two problems: first, how do they define and record the crimes and secondly, are the inspectors looking for increases or decreases? (It sounds obvious but one of the issues about confidence in the police was the readiness of the public to report things. Some would maintain that an increase was positive, at least initially.) In practice, what frontline coppers learned was that anything recorded as a burglary or robbery would have their bosses and checkers crawling all over it. It became clear that the government wanted to see the levels of crime go down and two features became endemic – distortion of how they recorded crime and the huge resources put into checking and double checking. So, in one force area, when an integral garage was broken into, and stuff taken (primarily from the car) this was recorded as 'theft from motor vehicle'. This obviated the need to record it as a burglary, which common sense says it was, but to which Her Majesty's Inspectorate of Constabulary (HMIC)would have paid attention and put the force under the spotlight. Another common distortion was that when burglars tried to force entry but failed this was put down as 'criminal damage' rather than attempted burglary. Every force had its variations on this theme but the outcome was a huge distortion in crime figures, intelligence systems filled with inaccurate information and frontline coppers knowing that they were being forced to do stupid things.

Police officers, like most frontline public sector people, are conscientious and vocationally minded. They like to feel they are doing the right things. The following example typifies the perverted logic they had been asked to enforce. Blunkett's regime asked police officers to be rigorous in recording and prosecuting any crime they spotted (it had a sensible logic but with the usual unintended consequences). A friend of mine spotted a pair of youths parking their bicycles outside his garage and breaking in. He challenged them and they ran off leaving their cycles behind. Naturally, assuming that they might return for them, he took the precaution of picking up a baseball bat. When the police arrived the culprits were long gone but on spotting the baseball bat, the only action the police were interested in was arresting him for carrying an offensive weapon. In another example, a man was clearing his mother's house after her death and found a sword under her bed. He took it to a police station to hand it in and was promptly arrested for, again, carrying an offensive weapon[1].

Meanwhile, in the back rooms, the activity was check, double check and treble check that their definitions of the crimes would comply with the Home Office regime. The only feedback the officers received was about how they had recorded the crime not about how well they had handled it. Imagine what that does to the commitment, attitude and behaviour of a workforce? The sheer waste of time was criminal in itself – we counted around 100 full time officers in one larger force doing nothing but checking crime records. This mess was compounded later by the government deciding that antisocial behaviour, race and violence were significant issues and that simply recording the crimes was insufficient. The police would also have to record these sorts of 'incidents'. The system is still in place and is so arcane that only an expert can use it.

Most forces need experienced back-room officers on permanent duty to check and amend the records to ensure compliance as well as ensuring that the force would pass the next HMIC inspection. The public were not slow in working out what the police paid attention to and they would report anything as a race issue, say, simply to ensure a quick and attentive response. Not only did this waste huge amounts of police time, as well as causing endless frustration, but it obviously made a nonsense of the recording system (on which the politicians rely to answer questions in the House). Furthermore, the police naturally came to regard the public as mendacious and frivolous, which is not a healthy relationship when one of the very worthy tenets of British policing is that policing is with the consent of the populace.

The stupidity, waste and damage of this logic was most clearly illustrated to me when the Home Office (after Sir Ronnie Flanagan's report) belatedly realised that it had inadvertently expunged the notion of 'discretion' from the police lexicon and needed to rediscover it. The real basis of good policing that had previously been the core of all force training is the need for officers to use their experience and common sense to do the right thing by and for the citizen. Four forces conducted pilot activities (giving officers their brains back was obviously not an easy choice). The direction from the Home Office was that 'violent (including domestic) and racial' incidents and crimes were to be excluded from the trial. In other words, 'you can use your brain but not if it's a violent or racial matter'.

---

1 Later there was a sharp rise in complaints against the police, mainly to do with uncivil behaviour. I would maintain that if you ask frontline coppers to do stupid things and have them explain that to the public, they are going to get frustrated at being made to look stupid. The only surprise is that they were as civil as they were!

Embedded logic

In our early days we noticed that people simply switched off when targets were removed. Targets made it only too obvious that things had not been achieved. So given that there was a culture of being paid attention to for what wasn't working, when the targets were removed the fear of being found failing remained.

We learned quickly that we had to replace targets with a better way of measuring work, and public sector managers should take note of this – simply taking the targets away results in a range of poor outcomes, because the culture is so embedded.

- Some will switch off. As noted earlier, when targets were removed, some police officers said, 'we don't have to pay attention to detections anymore', i.e. not only do we not measure the target but the activity no longer matters. We and the senior officers have actually had to say, 'no, you've still got to catch the bad guys!'

- Some get understandably emotional, feeling vulnerable because their security has been taken away.

- The politics of the work place is turned on its head. Managers like to spot good and bad performers and people must be defined as one or the other. So the people who make the targets – the apparently good performers – can suddenly become suspect (they might have been working the system) and some who had not, and appear to embody the new requirements, can now be seen as unlikely heroes.

- The leaders tell everyone that targets are no longer the currency. Junior managers, however, continue to use them for their own security – it is the only way they know they are succeeding. The only other option is a vacuum. As the leaders seldom get out of their offices into the work they never spot the problem.

It is no wonder that the public sector is not a happy place to work. Vocationally-minded people who signed up to help are finding themselves manipulating their work just to suit the targets. This is one case where the word 'stress' is only too appropriate.

A final component of this systemic problem is the role of 'performance management'. Performance management replaced the annual appraisal. Initially, it was a simple annual meeting that focused on setting and reviewing overall objectives for the individual and looking to future development and any training that might be relevant. Now, the target culture has hijacked performance management and, happily for the target obsessed, moved to more frequent 'one–to–ones' to be consolidated in the annual appraisal. The focus moved from 'general objectives' to 'how can we 'help' you make your targets?' The one-to-ones became exclusively numbers-focused and employees were in no doubt as to what 'good' looked like – make the numbers.

Performance improvement at any level and by any activity was focused on improving the numbers not improving the system. The presence of targets actually stops people doing the right things. The important task is to meet the target – doing the right thing would mean extra work. Citizens are also a problem in such a system because they are very likely to make it difficult for people to meet their targets. The target culture taught employees to hate the citizen while at the same time telling frontline employees to 'love the customer'.

Pavlov[2] is known for stimulus response experiments with dogs whereby he associated food with a bell and then found that the dog would salivate any time the bell was rung. He also ran experiments that gradually made the stimuli so similar that the dog could not discriminate and was randomly punished and rewarded (i.e. to the dog, totally unpredictably). Pavlov observed what he described as neurotic behaviour. This is what we are doing to our public sector employees.

---

2 Pavlov, Ian Petrovich. www.nobelprize.org/nobel_prizes/medicine/laureates/1904/pavlov–bio. html

Chapter 9

Getting value for money

One of Adam Smith's key concepts was achieving manufacturing efficiency through mass production. This method of reducing the cost of production is embedded in every aspect of economics in the western world.

It is not difficult to see why politicians would want to keep to this template. They want to be able to say that they are spending public money wisely and they want to have spare money to spend on whatever schemes they think will benefit the country. This is not unreasonable. If the public sees money is being spent well then they will feel less aggrieved at parting with their taxes.

The lamentable history of public spending has less to do with incompetent politicians and more to do with the design of the mass production system. One of the most significant aspects of the design that contributes to a lack of efficiency in the public sector is at the core of Smith's argument – the division of labour. Division of labour, as a practice, has created horizontal and vertical fragmentation. Work is divided into separate functions end to end, including that of management, which is divided into a range of specialist functions such as finance, HR, marketing, sales, IT and anything else seen as 'useful'. A fundamental set of problems lies in this 'management factory'.

One significant problem is that the true purpose of the organisation is obscured. This is a critical point. Every organisation should be driven by its purpose and that purpose should be defined by why it is needed by its citizens in the public sector and its customers in the private sector. What does it do from that perspective, what needs are being met and what problems are being solved? But it's often difficult to find any purpose other than to keep the management factory happy by 'making the numbers', 'meeting the targets'. IT systems, for example, are usually designed from the perspective of what information the managers need (in order to know whether they are or are not on track to make the numbers). How well they are doing in delivering what matters comes a poor second. Managers are rewarded for making the right numbers not doing good things. As long as they get their daily, weekly and monthly management reports they can feel in control. The presentation of these reports has become ever more refined with 'dashboards' and 'traffic lights' that highlight where action needs to be focused. Yet, these numbers are only ever a poor representation of reality. And the politicians being two steps away from the work have to suffer even further distortion as the data travels through the civil service departments.

It isn't just that it's poor data; it is what everyone believes to be knowledge. It is the stuff that drives decisions and the stuff that controls how we spend money. There are systemic reasons for this, all with their roots in Smith's logic: the purpose of division of labour was to achieve efficiency through economy of scale. I cannot overemphasise the centrality of this idea. It has become a western truism. Cut any manager open and you will find it at his or her core like a stick of rock.

Transactions

I need to introduce the idea of a transaction. In Smith's pin making example, there are sub-tasks into which production is split – drawing the wire, cutting the wire, pointing one end, etc. The simpler and more repetitive the task, the easier it was to employ anyone off the street. This is the essence of division of labour. Assuming that everything you make you can sell, then higher volumes combined with ever increasing productivity will lead to economy of scale. This was one of the key elements of Henry Ford's workers' system – he was able to take illiterate, often immigrant labour and make them productive in a very short time. Ford added the assembly line – the mechanisation of the process. He always maintained that it was the advent of electricity that allowed him to do this – being able to move the work past the operators and have each operator equipped with power tools. This was what became called mass production but it was a natural extension of the remorseless hunt for productivity.

Look at any public, private or even voluntary sector organisation today and you will see the same thing. Work has been split into transactions and grouped into functions, horizontal and vertical. The vertical separation of functions means that managers never see the front line and their 'theory of organisation' is never challenged – the fiction lives on.

The first problem with the notion of a transaction is that, by definition, it relates to only a small amount of activity, and this immediately undermines knowledge of the system as a whole. We have knowledge of each bit but nothing to tell us how the whole is working from end to end. Economy of scale, don't forget, is a remorseless logic that dictates standardisation of transactions followed by a constant pursuit of cheaper ways of carrying out each transaction. It persists through the fiction that if you add all the savings together there will be overall savings. The flaw in the logic is that if the goal is to reduce cost, there is no evaluation of the overall purpose of what is being done. As long as each operation is cheaper over time the goal is met. Even in the private sector the problem is ever present. A telecoms company decided to outsource the customer service call centre to India. The UK management also decided that the easy way to reduce the cost of each transaction was to automate the service by putting the diagnostic routines on the web. When the broadband service failed, as it did for me, I contacted the organisation and was answered by an agent in India. Needless to say the web-based support, even if it had been helpful, wasn't available because my system wasn't working. It was apparent that, however bright and helpful the personnel were, they had been given a job called, 'adhere to service standards,' rather than, 'fix the customer's problem'. This was evident to me by the number of calls I received from them asking me if the agent I had spoken to on the previous call had done X, Y and Z. They would also ask if my issue had been resolved but when I said no, they were clearly unable to do anything about it.

Fifteen outbound calls, thirty-five inbound calls, a service engineer and six elapsed days failed to resolve the problem. I resorted to displacement behaviour and called anyone I could. Somehow I managed to find a person in the company who took pity on me and connected me to the UK broadband expert (his number was pin protected – god forbid that the customer could ever speak to an expert). He solved my problem in 20 seconds. He was, however, so bored, had so little to do and his expertise underused, that it took me fifteen minutes to get him off the line.

The primary question this raises is, 'how could managers in this company believe that one 20 second phone call to an expert was more expensive than 50 calls to and from India?' This is the nub of the economic failure of economy of scale. Managers split the work into transactions and, somehow, by standardising the response and combining all the transactions, imagine that the organisation will be able to meet its purpose from the customer or citizen perspective. Each transaction has its own measure and the system implicitly assumes that if each measure is met, the overall purpose will be met. In practice, the managers only achieve a feeling that they are in control. There is no measure of purpose from the customer's perspective. It would have been helpful if there had been a measure of how often and how quickly they resolved problems for customers (i.e. such that the customer would say the problem was resolved). I was in one of the same company's call centres in the UK and was encouraged when I saw a very visible number on the wall telling everyone that 95% of customer issues were resolved first time. However, when we listened to calls it was obvious that almost no customer issue was resolved. Indeed, the purpose of the call centre was to refer issues to an engineering unit and resolution for the customer was, by definition, impossible. But managers would see the '95% issues resolved' and would have no reason to doubt it.

This was also evident in a pensions company we worked with who outsourced all their pension advice to India. Pensioners called a UK number, their query was logged and sent to India. India could only answer 20% of the queries and shipped the rest back. The UK cleaned up what they could and sent them back to India. This cycle was repeated 3 or 4 times. It took anything from up to 4 months to resolve a query. As an experiment, they put an expert at the front line in the UK and almost every query was resolved in less than twenty minutes.

The system was measuring transaction costs: first the cost of the phone call and then the cost of the back office function. Most service organisations have back office functions now. Even police forces talk about having back office functions. They have arisen alongside, or rather behind, the call centre. Because the call centre is measured on the efficiency with which it handles calls (time to answer, talk time, etc.) any work that goes into resolving anything remotely complicated is seen as interfering with the call taker's efficiency. Therefore a whole new function, the back office, has had to be created to handle the work. Over time, it is quite normal for the call centre to become a referral point for various back offices. In reality, the work could have been done once at first point of contact but is now done in several different places, significantly increasing the probability of delay and error.

There was no data about what it cost to resolve a pensioner query. How then, could they make a sensible decision about outsourcing it anywhere? Yet these decisions are being made all the time.

Knowledge is no better in the public sector. I was involved briefly in a logistics activity with the Ministry of Defence (MoD). I watched pallets being put on aircraft for shipment abroad. I was told that no fewer than fifteen separate organisations across the UK had been involved in processing the 'order'. It was a simple task: the military says, 'we need this much of X, here', and the system has to find it and ship it. What would be the best way to test that such a system was working? The answer is to is test whether it achieves its purpose: measure how often the orders turn up where and when they are needed and whether they are usable when they come off the transport. Then find out what that costs. No-one I worked with had that data and they did not believe anyone else had it either.

What this shows, then, is that if there is no data about achieving true purpose it is impossible to make economic decisions about better ways of doing things. Put simply, if you don't know the cost of doing something, then how do you know that any other way of doing it is cheaper?

Probably the most incontrovertible truth that we have learned is that no mass production organisation we have come across knows the true cost of doing anything. Yet, thousands of bright, well-intentioned managers are behaving as though they do.

Understanding the cost to the system

Meanwhile, consider the budget process. The CEO of the public or private organisation has a budget. That budget is subdivided across the functions and departments such that if each comes in on cost then the system is sound and everyone can sleep at night. What the system does not know, as we have seen, is whether it is meeting purpose. If the system does not know if it is meeting purpose (i.e. it has no data) then how can it know if all the work done is purposeful? Furthermore, with costs split across departments, no one budget holder will know the true cost of doing anything, let alone anything purposeful.

In the pensions company above, the assumption was, as it is in the public sector, that a 'back office/front office' split is essential so that people who answer the phone are not interrupted. (The interruption is not seen as damaging to the customer but to the productivity data – staff will be more productive if they can concentrate on one task and not be interrupted.) It is a 'cost of doing business' and therefore unavoidable, goes the logic. It is a symptom of this stupidity that the concept of front and back office arose in the first place: front office takes the calls and then passes the work to the back office where the work is processed. This is nothing more than a work creation system, making two jobs out of one. Imagine the call centre of the pensions company. If it takes up to 3 months to resolve a query, how many calls are coming in that sound like the following: 'I haven't heard anything', 'I sent you this but you keep asking for it again', 'you've sent me this but I don't think you've answered my question'. Who, in that pension company system, has the responsibility to test the system to see if it meets purpose? Who would spot anything other than a team not meeting budget or service quality standards? Who would spot that many, if not most, of the calls would be unnecessary if the system were designed differently? Economy of scale logic treats each piece of work as a unit of production to be measured and standardised. When the CEO understood the flow of the work and understood the waste designed into the process, he immediately set about returning the work to the UK.

Private and public sector organisations have outsourced large amounts of work. Consider outsourcing a call centre. In the private sector anything from 40 – 80% of calls are preventable (80% is not untypical). In the public sector, it is lower but still 30 – 60% percent. The typical outsource deal is to pay per transaction, e.g. £2 per call. The more the system is run on mass production lines, the more predictable are the failures and the more you pay the outsourcer for handling calls that should not have been necessary in the first place. If the calls are preventable then much of the 'front office' work is also preventable. The goal is productivity and yet the logic produces a system where members of staff are expected to process more and more rubbish productively – faster garbage. Huge amounts of the public sector are being outsourced to achieve so called efficiency and service improvement: call centres, care for the elderly, transport, IT and HR support, police forensics and translation services and much more. Does anyone know how much waste is being outsourced?

The inescapable conclusion is: fragmentation, hierarchy and splitting work into transactions ensures a lack of useful knowledge, does nothing but make work non-purposeful and is very expensive. This is the logic that underpins economy of scale.

In case you think that this might be just a service sector problem, consider the General Motors story of last century. A particular vehicle proved to have a predictable oil leak from the engine. After much research, the engine manufacturing team tracked the problem to an 'O' ring between the transmission and the engine. The seal cost a few cents and the better quality seal that would solve the problem cost a few cents more. The part in question, however, was technically in the transmission and the manager of the transmission function did not want his budget 'blown' by the extra cost so the problem was not fixed.

But we might want to argue that the waste and inefficiency of fragmented work is not inevitable and that once we know the problems we can manage them better – find better measures, employ managers who visit each other's departments and take a view on purpose and who maybe spend more time in the front line. Maybe we have to be smarter and do the same things but in a better way? Surely economy of scale can't be that wrong? Well it is difficult to say categorically that it is wrong. In all the businesses we have so far been involved with, including manufacturing, it has proven to be an unhelpful goal and one that obscures cost and failure for customers. However, it is such a truism for managers that it is usually not worth having the debate. A better position is to say that economy of flow – looking to make everything work well from end to end is a much better goal in service and, as in Toyota, manufacturing too.

Budgets are controlled department by department so managers/ministers seek cost savings bit by bit. But as no one knows the true cost of doing anything, it's very difficult to make sensible decisions about how to do it cheaper. Managers can only reduce the cost of transactions rather than whole functions. The methods are typically: standardise the transactions, replace the people with IT and ship off-shore or to specialist mass processors. This is a rarely challenged logic. It is such a truism that governments have built it into the design of most public sector systems. The citizen, irrespective of their need or problem, will tend to receive a standardised offering – a commodity, simple and repeatable and often out-sourced. All too frequently, the problem is only resolved when someone in the organisation takes responsibility and manages the case. But this is usually rectification rather than the first response. This already shows the fallacy of the economy of scale logic – it must be cheaper to get things right first than to keep rectifying problems afterwards.

In the service sector, the notion of standardised units is always problematic. It implies that all customers are the same and the same response will meet all needs. It takes little thought to realise how stupid that is. People do not always have simple needs that can be resolved by a simple transaction. How, then, can a unit-cost-driven standardised system meet such varied/complex needs and what happens if it does not? The answers, as we have seen, should be obvious – a) it cannot and b) much failure and huge cost – and very frustrated customers.

The logic is the same in the public sector. They know the cost of a transaction but not the cost of the whole process. An example: I went for an MRI scan recently as part of a wider investigation. I'd had a biopsy and they said to leave the MRI until after the tissue had settled down from the biopsy damage. That meant a month delay to my diagnosis and a lot of worry. It became obvious later that they knew I would need an MRI so I asked why they hadn't done the MRI first? 'Ah well', came the reply, 'MRIs are very expensive so we try not to overuse it'. You could see immediately that the system was being run on transaction cost logic. They plan and ration the use according to the cost of an MRI scan rather than how important it is in the diagnostic flow. And yet when I'd had the MRI, I'd asked the operator what percentage of scans she thought were necessary and how many were done 'because they could'. Her view was that 60% were unnecessary. This happens because procedures dictate when to use the MRI scans rather than anyone looking end-to-end to see what works and what is really necessary.

The number of other tests I've had that appear to have no purpose is mounting. A colleague did some work for a hospital pathology lab and confirmed that a high number of tests were pointless; simply ticking boxes or re-tests for out-of-date tests. The NHS could probably save the 4% that government has determined it must, purely by understanding patient flow from end to end, i.e. from the time a patient first presents to the time treatment is complete. No one person manages the flow or makes decisions. It is left to the 'system' and therefore to procedures and tick boxes to control. The waste is extraordinary.

The police are trying to outsource all sorts of services, 'to reduce unit cost' (Ian Blair's words). The emotion raised about privatising the public sector is to miss the point. Running services from an economy of scale perspective ensures that there is little useful knowledge about how the system works. Custody is a regular topic because it is seen as a transaction – arrest people, keep them safe and process them. If you do the sums and work out how many people are in custody and at what times of day and week then you can devise a simple contract with costs per arrest/detention. So goes the logic. No one asks what the purpose of custody is as part of an investigation process. You will not see the data about how badly investigation processes are carried out and the large number of people who really do not need to be in custody in the first place. If you could see the data you would then be able to decide whether outsourcing part of an investigation flow is likely to improve or detract from the outcomes.

In the 80s, police services started to close stations and in the 90s Tony Blair's Home Secretaries gave further emphasis to call centres. What the police lost was local knowledge – the most vital commodity it could ever have. The local sergeant had been the corner stone of knowledge and relationships. So, when Blunkett suddenly rediscovered 'neighbourhood policing' (was there ever anything else?) policing had to rediscover local knowledge. It still hasn't. There are more police officers than ever before, there have been billions spent on IT to host, among other things, intelligence systems but still there is no local knowledge except in the heads of a few good officers. Their knowledge, we have discovered, rarely finds its way into the intelligence system. We have no idea, and neither do they, how much has been spent trying to recreate local knowledge and relationships.

What's more, the simple telephone conversation that was supposed to replace the local bobby is a very poor substitute. Very few callers' issues are resolved. The call, in practice, simply sets up a chain of tasks such as visits or appointments. Often the main work for neighbourhood officers is carrying out the task delegated by the call centre. The call centre often appears to run the force rather than the other way round. How much does all this referring of work cost?

The government of the day, as any current government would, sought to make it easy for citizens to contact the police. (The goal was always ease of contact. It was assumed that this would lead to resolution of issues but this was not designed in or tested – the target was speed of answering.) At the same time they wanted to make sure that the 999 number was not overwhelmed – it had at least been understood that citizens would call 999 as the easiest way of getting response from the emergency services, whatever the issue. A new simple non-emergency number, 101, was trialled in three forces. When the 101 number was introduced it was such a politically important scheme that forces ensured that it was fully resourced. Where that was the case, the public loved it – they were getting what they should have been getting from the real police service. All that had happened was that forces had had to duplicate their service, creating, in effect, a separate neighbourhood team for the 101 service.

The public sector should be designed to do whatever it is that matters to people, to do it in the first instance, and as soon as is required. They should measure their capability to resolve issues fully and how long it takes them to do so.

Reducing cost through commissioning – the market

Recent governments have decided that relying on the market is a way of reducing cost. They talk about choice as an important component – the customer chooses the best supplier, which then thrives at the cost of less good suppliers. A range of commissioning organisations has been set up to specify these services and allow suppliers to compete for them. On the face of it this could be seen as a positive self-regulating mechanism.

In practice, however, this is fundamentally flawed and produces high-cost services that do not solve the citizens' problems. The flaws are not those which most commentators will identify, i.e. privatising the public sector and lack of accountability. They are, first, that customers do not want choice, they simply want what they want (and want it to work). More importantly, in a true market you are competing to provide what customers want to buy. In the public sector it is the politicians who have decided what customers want and how, therefore, the services are to be specified. (There is a serious problem with treating citizens as 'customers', which I shall pick up later.)

Mass production thinkers will split any service into transactions and specify the activity for each transaction. For example, the Meals On Wheels service is commissioned in County X. The organisation that has the best track record and widest existing network actually wins the contract. So far so good. What the contract specifies is 'delivering the meals'. What has been lost as a result is the real value of the delivery service in looking after the people receiving the meals. Every driver was used to making sure people were well and had what they needed. Now, if there is a problem they have to report it to another commissioned service rather than doing what they always did – to help people there and then. Think about that from the perspective of the volunteer; why they chose to do it and the value that they contributed. The turnover in volunteers has gone up, the costs have gone up and corners are being cut. The overall cost will go up as we now have multiple services doing what one used to do and that even assumes that the multiple services actually do what the original service did.

Second, commissioning seeks to provide the same standardised services wherever they are commissioned. In the same county as the Meals On Wheels contract, a small local charity had built a very clever business that essentially brokered relationships between people needing 'odd jobs' doing and tradesmen. The agency connected local people – helping in the garden, a bit of decorating, shopping, etc. – and was cheaper than any other competing service, even the other charities. It fostered local relationships without an intervening bureaucracy. The County Council learned of this success and wanted to 'scale it', i.e. spread it across the county. Needless to say, it was commissioned and a large contractor took it on as just another 'odd job' services contract. Most of the true value was lost and costs went up. As costs rise who pays? The citizen.

I was working with a provider of domiciliary care who was (and is) paid by the hour to care for individuals. We conducted an in-depth review of how the service was performing and tested a new approach based on helping their clients to live well, rather than just delivering the specified visits at the specified times to do the specified tasks. The results were compelling. Citizens were delighted by how personal and helpful the service had become. Carers loved the fact that they were making a real difference and had freedom to make decisions about who they should prioritise spending time with, how long they should take and what they should do with that time, i.e. what mattered to the person receiving the care. Carers also learned what it meant to be a team, providing cover for each other, liaising to ensure that the people they were responsible for were getting the absolute best from them. They were no longer simply going out as isolated individuals to deliver their personal roster of tasks. The amount of sickness dropped. Failure demand disappeared. Most striking was that citizens largely stopped consuming other services, so much so that one local GP commented that he thought that some of his patients must have died because he hadn't seen them in so long. They weren't dead. They had just been helped.

The provider had learned that in order to be effective and efficient the team needed to:

- Ignore the scope of the service they were commissioned to supply in order to help with whatever was needed.
- Ignore what the social work assessment said and spend longer than before conducting a 'getting to know each other' process with citizens.
- Work on a geographical basis so that time could be flexed efficiently around the needs of the citizens.

There were many more points of learning but these three provoked the biggest immune response from the commissioners because they directly challenged the pre-existing management controls in the system. This new service didn't fit their specification. The social work assessment was considered a cost and quality control mechanism (itself subject to other cost and quality control mechanisms like the social care 'panel'). A lot of time, cost and expertise had gone into ensuring that the micro-commissioning decision of 'this care for that person' was right. It wasn't proper to have care providers ignoring this and 'writing themselves blank cheques' (i.e. making decisions about what help was needed, by who and when). Most of all though, it just wasn't acceptable to suggest that a whole geography should be managed by one care provider because that, it was argued, would contradict the principle of choice. What if Mrs Jones at number 27 didn't want her care from them?

So this is what it came down to. Offering a choice of provider was more important than providing help. Unit cost was more important than end-to-end cost. Decision-making couldn't be at the interface between the citizen and the provider, only at the interface between the citizen and the micro-commissioner (the social worker in this instance). Commissioning was now about setting the framework to guard against 'what ifs' rather than about collaboratively providing what mattered to the person. Interestingly, providing what matter to individuals could save the local system several million pounds in recurrent annual spend if it were adopted across the county, and everyone who had experienced it loved it.

What we see is a spiralling failure built on the commissioning logic: the commissioners specify the services and design the contracts accordingly. The specification is based on all sorts of plausible logic but not what matters to the citizen. The services fail to solve citizens' problems and so ever more needs are created that will, in turn, not be solved. The cost is an issue but so is the trust between the citizen and the state. It will also reinforce plausible but unhelpful notions such as the 'ever spiralling cost of care for older people'. Designed this way it will most certainly spiral and we will never know the true cost.

The evidence is overwhelming and yet no-one sees it. Everyone is trapped in a framework of logic and information that maintains the plausibility of the current system. Money is being wasted, citizens receive services that do not work, employees are forced to do stupid things that sap their morale and create high levels of complaints that soak up resources. What's more, this logic puts people at risk of harm while purporting to keep us safe, as the next chapter will show.

Chapter 10

Keep us safe

The world is seen to be a risky place. It is risky for the citizen who is exposed to public services and for the professionals who either fail to deliver or create actual harm! It is much more risky for the professionals because they can be brutally exposed by the news and social media. It is also risky for the politicians who face equally brutal exposure and are usually encouraged to fall on their swords.

But how do we manage risk?

The command and control logic of the mass production system is based on leading from the top. The traditional method is to specify procedures and then inspect for compliance. The manager's solace is knowing that the procedures are in place and that everyone is following them. The implicit comfort is that nothing can go wrong and, even if it did, he or she cannot be accused of negligence. In the public sector, the system is similarly protected from risk when it is shown to be compliant with the specified procedures – managers, politicians and anyone else can say, 'we cannot be blamed for doing everything our procedures required of us'. How many times do we hear the defence, 'our procedures were fully compliant with the laid down requirements'. The cynics among us shout, 'well that's alright then'. The truth is that the procedures don't work, haven't worked before and will not work from here on in, but it remains a credible defence. Why? I think even the politicians recognise the feebleness of saying, 'we must learn lessons' when they clearly don't. There is always the bit in parentheses, (until the next time). If we ask only: 'Did they comply?', then what do we learn?

The question should be, 'Do procedures protect us from risk even if properly policed?' The answer is an unequivocal, no. The only protection against risk is knowledge. You need to know what the risk is, how it works, why and so on; and what are the causes and probabilities and how would we know? That knowledge can only come from those close to the issue, understanding what they are faced with and from those who have faced similar problems and have collected and collated knowledge in the past. Just how much can we protect people anyway?

How do we know if the procedures were appropriate or capable of being generalised? The people responsible for managing risk in this system are the specifiers and those who send out the inspectors. They are, by definition, not close to the action and have no means of generating or testing knowledge to truly understand the problems they are trying to prevent.

There is another problem here. Even if the procedural approach is right, and the specifiers are responsible for creating the procedures, then it follows that the people doing the work cannot be responsible for the outcomes. If you decide how I work then it is you, not me, who is responsible for the quality of my work. As the people doing the work no longer have the responsibility, then the likelihood of existing and new problems increases and with it the probable 'need' (in the eyes of the specifiers) for new procedures. What is, and always will be, axiomatic is that people who are responsible must be the people on the spot who can take action based on their knowledge and judgement. In the current system, these people have no responsibility.

We have seen this in operation for the last twenty years. The sense of responsibility that public sector professionals and operators had always shown has been eroded significantly. It becomes obvious when you ask the simple question, 'What do managers pay attention to?' Although there is much debate about what Deming did and did not say he makes a remark in one of his videos to the effect: 'tell me what you're going to count and I'll tell you what I'll do'.

Public sector managers have, for some time, paid attention to two things only:

1) How well are we doing against the targets?

2) Are we complying with our inspection regime? (The inspection regime has a simple logic: you tell us what your procedures are and we will inspect against them.)

The implicit message is: 'don't use your brain or your common sense, just make sure we are compliant – that way we are safe. They can't get us if we're compliant'.

The last decades have also seen a rise in general legislation: health and safety itself, human rights, data protection and equality. Failure to comply does not simply mean an inspection failure but prosecution.

Collectively this has led to a culture of 'make sure we pass our inspections' which in turn has led to a gold plating of procedures. It is no exaggeration to state that in many public sector organisations you would easily believe that the purpose was 'be safe'. I sat in a County Council call centre one January recently. Most of the calls were about pot holes but the next largest category was calls from people asking what could be done to help elderly parents who were starting to struggle to live unaided. The response, very politely, was, 'we can't talk to you, it's confidential, we can only talk to the person concerned'. It illustrated the 'be safe' principle only too clearly. Confidentiality was seen as more important than helping someone.

When frontline people are able to use their judgement they can assess the risk case by case and, in principle as well as mostly in practice, reduce and prevent risk. As it is, not only is each professional following procedures but each agency will have separate procedures that will inevitably be at odds with each other. It is more accurate to say that the system is designed not to spot risk. My brother works for Age UK and in his experience it is not unusual for relatives to take financial advantage of vulnerable people. It is a valid concern. The knowledge required to protect vulnerable people is going to come from those who support the person talking to each other and being in a system that encourages those caring for people to act on that knowledge. As it is they are concerned to cover their backs and be seen to be safe – rather than keep others safe.

The same problem has developed in the health sector where an increasing number of scandals is being exposed. Again it is worth contrasting knowledge with procedures. GPs used to know their patients, the individuals, the families and family histories. They would know likely problems, useful tests and, above all, they could see the differences over time. They have now, since the renegotiation of their contract that limits contact, especially out of hours, all but ceded that knowledge apart from the hard core of regular patients. It is now highly probable that the GP is not the first person to see the patient in extremis – it will be A&E, or a paramedic or a locum. These practitioners will have some transactional knowledge in the IT system but even assuming that this is up to date and accurate, it is a poor substitute for knowing the person. Even in the limited time we have spent in the health sector we have come across many missed or poor diagnoses which have led to serious harm to the patient. The practitioners have no context – all they can do is run as many tests as they can and hope to spot the problem. They are then measured on whether they carried out reasonable procedures. The practitioners only ever do their best, but the system is designed around the wrong assumptions – procedures can never protect against risk. A young GP was telling me recently that GPs and hospital doctors routinely commission a battery of tests regardless. All too often, she says, there is no need for any tests.

In practice this creates a difficult dilemma for government. Do they trust the professionals or do they control them? Ministers are generally aware of the history of doing both and are genuinely, in my experience, unhappy doing either. As long as the ridiculous debate remains, 'can we or can't we trust the professionals?' then nothing will be resolved. What's more, risk will increase as procedures are used to control events and people instead of having the right people in the right place to do the job properly. In principle this means having the right expert at first point of contact. As ever, knowledge is the key.

Whistleblowing in the health service is a good example of the dilemma. Governments have been encouraging professionals to highlight poor and dangerous practice on the basis that fellow professionals are more likely to spot it. Tony Blair refined the 1998 Public Interest Disclosure Act following scandalous treatment of doctors and consultants who had chosen to go public after their bosses had failed to act. Nothing has changed and even the Department of Health has been singularly ineffective in supporting such whistleblowers. At one level it is hard to see why, after the likes of Shipman and the Bristol heart surgery cases, anyone could fail to see the case to be made. But it continues to be an abject failure. In practice, whistleblowing should be a last resort. Practitioners should be able to highlight problems and risks as they find them. But the way the professions are managed and manage themselves has made that impossible. The treatment of whistleblowers sends a general message throughout every organisation – 'keep quiet and follow procedures'. There is no reward; only the danger in drawing attention to yourself.

In contrast to this, and a system often aspired to by the health professions, is the 'near miss' system operated by the aviation sector, both civil and military. For decades, pilots have willingly subscribed to an anonymous recording system where the explicit intention is to learn from mistakes. They are only too aware that pilot error is the main cause of accidents but they also realise the systemic benefits of analysis and the relationship between pilots, technology and procedures. This system arose from the grass roots, not the management or political cadres. I recall working with an aircraft engineer whose regular pub companion was his GP. The GP would complain on a bad day about his responsibility, "many of my decisions can mean life or death". The engineer's retort was, "many of my decisions mean several hundred lives or deaths".

We seem to have the worst of all worlds. Government puts faith in technology and procedures to protect us from risk and this creates what is now known as 'moral hazard' whereby we are encouraged to feel safe because of the technology and procedures. We fail to look for risk. Meanwhile the public sector is paralysed by a sense that it must be safe above all else and not only fails to see true purpose as a consequence, but is manifestly unsafe.

Risk can only be managed successfully by frontline people who have knowledge, and who can talk easily to each other in whatever agency, knowing that the management of the risk is all that matters. For example, if the police and social services can share knowledge on the spot instead of going through committees and referral processes, much could be done better.

Chapter 11

The citizen's relationship with the state

It seems to be an accepted principle today that the market will help to improve public services. This thinking is driven by ministers' frustration with what they see as 'public sector mentality' – a lack of initiative and business sense – and they assume that competition will provide better value for money.

In order to justify the use of the market in the public sector, politicians of all stripes have created the notion that the citizen needs choice – choice of school, hospital, care provider, and so on. But is this true? I mentioned earlier that the market is a false concept in the public sector because it is not citizens but politicians who decide what to purchase. Public services are not lifestyle choices or discretionary services, they are solutions to problems. In Herzberg's terms, they are hygiene factors – things that are necessary rather than desirable. When I'm ill I want to be cured, when my bins need emptying I want it done regularly and on time and when I'm burgled I want the burglar caught. All that matters to me is that the service works when I need it. I want a good school nearby, a good hospital nearby, an effective police force nearby. I don't want choice, I want something that works.

McKnight and Block[1] make a cogent argument to reveal another more corrosive consequence of market logic in the public sector. The market converts the citizen into a 'customer'. Indeed, in recent decades, UK governments and public sector agencies openly describe their citizens as customers. Customer service is an avowed aim and has become a target set of behaviours for public sector agencies. It is certainly plausible and attractive. It appears beyond debate that you would want to be treated as a valued customer – who would not want a John Lewis or Marks and Spencer service from a public sector agency?

However, when you become a customer your relationship with the provider/supplier becomes contractual in nature – you expect to get what you have paid for and judge accordingly. The notion of 'customer' is the same as the 'consumer' and the consumer expects value for money – for which the responsibility is exclusively with the provider. The customer does not feel the need to be responsible for any part of the service. If the provider does not meet the expectations of the customers they feel fully entitled to complain.

---

1 McKnight and Block. (2010) *The Abundant Community*. Berrett-Koehler

Mcknight and Block describe the essence of the citizen as a consumer of public services: *In consumer society [..] functions are removed from the family and community and provided by the state*[2]. The citizen becomes increasingly dependent on the experts provided by the state (or putative market). And, if the citizen does not like what is on offer then the solution is always to purchase an alternative – consumers seek to buy their way out of problems. They can move house to a different neighbourhood, pay for a different school, GP or hospital consultant, pay for special needs support. The system works by giving the citizen choice and the services chosen are the ones that will survive.

The citizen expects local authorities to keep neighbourhoods clean and tidy, doctors to keep them healthy, care homes to look after their elderly and schools to educate and look after their children. McKnight and Block go so far as to say that in North America the state is implicitly telling citizens not to worry, the state will live their lives for them.

The government-imposed transfer of responsibility from citizen to state is one aspect of the problem. The corollary is the increasing professionalisation of the state. The citizen becomes ever more dependent on what professional medics, teachers and police officers can and will do, as well as what they can't and won't do. When those citizens are allowed to be consumers they can become critical about value for money and what they see as their rights. This places a burden of protection on the professional and the consequence is an arms race of rights versus protection. Even in the UK, GPs are paying thousands of pounds a year for very basic professional indemnity.

The degree to which the UK has travelled the route of consumerisation of public services compared with the US is debatable, but the signs are certainly there. The most obvious example is university education. Students are paying significant sums of money for their education. They are also complaining in ever increasing numbers about the quality of teaching. Whilst it is right that they should complain, it does beg the question as to how much responsibility for learning has shifted from student to university.

There is also the implicit assumption that students will choose the courses and universities that meet their needs and that market choice will therefore control and rationalise the system – bad courses and colleges will not survive.

Primary schools will be providing free meals for all pupils. On the one hand this can only be laudable but on the other, where is the notion of *in loco parentis* going to stop? Already, if children are not learning they are widely assumed to have special needs. Government policy is such that it is the schools that are responsible for identifying, funding and rectifying the

---

2 *ibid*

alleged need.

McKnight tells a story of visiting a youth centre in the USA where the walls are covered in flyers for activities. He sees the children sitting around and asks them what's going on. They tell him they are bored. It is obviously someone else's responsibility to entertain them – they have become consumers.

While the citizen is expected to exercise choice as a consumer, the responsibility for what choices one has is with the provider. The relationship is between citizen and state (provider) and the traditional citizen to citizen and citizen to community relationships begin to erode. During the riots of 2012 in the UK, there was an example of shopkeepers wanting to help each other protect their own shops. The police accused them of being vigilantes and made it clear that this was a job for professional police officers. There is a fine line to be drawn here but to deny property owners any responsibility for looking after their own property would not seem to be a good place to start.

Michael Oliver in the *British Medical Journal*, March 2009[3], described how the medical system is increasingly turning elderly people into patients. Although much debated recently, screening is generally held to be a good thing. However, the more you screen the more likely you are to find things. The test results will tick boxes and exceed predetermined thresholds and the people tested become patients to be prescribed drugs. Their role as patients is to behave themselves and comply with the regime. Oliver describes this as 'a bureaucratic demand for documentation that can lead to overdiagnosis'.

Similar patterns are discernible in the legal system. The law is there to formalise the way in which the citizen gains redress and justice after having been wronged by another. This is to obviate the need for the citizen to take the law into their own hands. However, we now see examples of people being prosecuted vicariously. A bystander overhears what they believe to be a racist remark, for example, and reports the person who is then arrested and potentially prosecuted. The prosecution takes place irrespective of whether the person assumed to be the victim feels aggrieved or not. This would seem to be the law being run for its own ends rather than for its true purpose of protecting us from others.

There is also law that protects us from ourselves. Whilst few would now argue with laws requiring seat belts, self-protection can be taken too far. For a recent milestone birthday my wife bought me a taxi ride in a famous WWll bomber aircraft. On arrival at the air field we had a mandatory, lengthy health and safety briefing. Afterwards I asked if it would not have been easier for a simple briefing and for us to have signed a disclaimer in

3 http://www.bmj.com/content/338/bmj.b873.extract?sid=e54b873d-ead3-4ae6-9ab3-93d58210a8c4

case we injured ourselves. 'No', came the answer. Their insurance company had decreed that in the eyes of the law we were assumed to be incapable of self-restraint in the face of overwhelming temptation. We were not allowed to be responsible for ourselves.

At the very least there is significant confusion as to what the citizen is and is not responsible for. I was a parish councillor and we needed to trim some branches from a tree in the graveyard. I assumed that we could simply convene a few able bodied people and do it ourselves. That may indeed have been the best option but I was soon warned off by my fellow councillors with talk of insurance requirements and risk assessments. We also had a problem with some children causing minor problems in the village. The conversation went back and forth between handling it ourselves or calling in the police. Many of us citizens simply do not have the confidence to know what we can and can't, should or should not do, for ourselves.

Whatever the precise state of the consumer versus citizen debate it raises important questions. How much responsibility should the citizen have for themselves and, therefore, what relationship should the state have with its citizenry? And do we want citizens as consumers?

If we want public services to be modelled on a consumer society then the cost of the government doing everything becomes unsustainable. The more the state does for the citizen the more the citizen will expect the state to do. If I am overweight or out of work, it is the state's responsibility. If the verge outside my house is untidy, if my neighbour or relative needs help, it is the state's responsibility. The debate then has to move either to rationing or to alternative methods of paying for services – higher tax or citizens paying direct. The market, and the current commissioning system, already designs services in a way that applies a price structure. It would be very simple to ask the citizen to pay rather than have government pick up the tab.

If citizens do take responsibility for themselves and do engage with their communities, however that may be defined, does the cost administration go down, do communities and their infrastructures work better, and are people better cared for and happier? The evidence from the work described in earlier chapters would indicate strongly that it is much cheaper to work with citizens who want to be responsible for themselves and their communities. It is arguable that cost is not the most important issue. There is an increasing focus on quality of life. This is also measurable.

McKnight and Block would argue that a consumer society is inherently unfulfilling and represents a poor quality of life for all. They describe the way consumerism isolates people. The tendency is to shift towards relationships with suppliers – when I need something, I buy it. Whilst this does not preclude family, friends and community, fewer people seek help from them, judging by the evidence they present from their studies in the US[4].

The citizen as a community player, by contrast, seeks to solve problems through a collaborative relationship with their community and family, with experts giving advice rather than direction. In this way, the relationship with government agencies is very different: the professional capability is one of support and one of augmenting the capabilities of the citizenry rather than supplanting it.

Another and important view about the citizen as community player versus citizen as consumer comes from recent psychological theory and experiments on reciprocity. This view has developed from evolutionary biology and understanding why humans cooperate. In principle, the learning describes people as willing collaborators on the basis that mutual support is better than individual endeavour over time. If we take a view that this is a predisposition then we can posit that the opportunity to contribute matters. However, there are rules. People will contribute only as long as they see others reciprocating. They also need their contribution acknowledged, so that reputation as a contributor is important. To the extent that this is true, it is far easier to achieve this in a local context where the reciprocators are known to one another. Where that is not the case, the individual is reliant on other agencies, the police or government, to punish the non-reciprocators. Hence one can understand much of the public anger towards the bankers who have taken rather than given, and have got away with it. Psychologists would describe this as part of the underpinnings of our sense of justice.

The logic is that citizens like to contribute but primarily with people known to them. This would also indicate that government activity, such as benefit distribution, is best done locally on the basis of perceived deservedness. The alternative picture, then, is the citizen as consumer has no reciprocal or contributing role and only deals with ever more centralised and anonymous distant supplies.

We need a debate as to what relationship we want with government and in the meantime we can collect evidence as to what works. What is the best way to contribute effective and cost-efficient provision of things that matter to people? Should we be concerned about quality of life and, if so, how does that relate to service provision?

The proposition to test, therefore, is whether citizens acting primarily as responsible for themselves, and collectively for their communities, provides for a better quality of life and lower cost of service provision.

---

4 *ibid*

Part Two Summary

Control

Politicians, above all, need to feel in control. They need to feel that they have control over daily outcomes in the public sector and over the mechanisms and direction of change, whenever that is politically necessary.

As I have outlined, they want to know that the right results are being achieved, that the public sector is good value for money, that they are not exposed to scandal and that citizens are safe. So strong is the fear of exposure that the *de facto* purpose of the public sector is 'be safe', long before there is any sense of delivering services. In addition to this, I believe that the biggest stumbling block to providing services is the erosion of the recognition of the responsible citizen. The government has painted itself into the position of living our lives for us – a most unhealthy and expensive outcome. It is, without doubt, a difficult problem.

Managing through the civil service and the professions is like performing surgery with boxing gloves on. When change is needed, there is a long delay before anything happens. Cause and effect are difficult to track, and even if politicians were minded to understand the consequences of their actions, it would often be hard to track.

However, that said, all these problems are compounded by the assumptions in public leadership at every level. They start at the top so we have to hold the politicians primarily responsible – as the saying goes, 'the fish rots from the head'.

The current assumptions are:

- Economy of scale maximises efficiency and reduces costs.
- The market (competition) will create value for money.
- Management through targets and budgets is efficient and effective.
- Functional design (putting boxes and labels around services) helps track effectiveness and efficiency.
- Designing and commissioning services will reduce cost and improve service through competitive tender.
- Holding managers and employees to account will improve performance (someone must be to blame).
- Reducing the cost of transactions will improve the overall cost.
- The manager's role is to deliver on targets and budget.

The current system is designed the way it is because these assumptions are believed to be true. What the citizen experiences, both in delivery and in taxation, is a direct consequence of this logic. In other words, the failures of the system are designed in. The fundamental problem and paradox is that everything is designed to reduce cost and yet this only results in driving cost up.

There is no doubt that this design is expensive and ineffective. While government and media seek to victimise employees for failure, the fact is that when success does occur it is often down to individuals doing their best to circumvent the system.

It is easy to say, and true to an extent, that politicians are unhappy with the system but simply can't see an alternative. Our experience, however, is that they are institutionally deaf to better solutions.

The 'Big Society' is a classic example of wanting a better outcome but with no idea of how to get there. The concept is hard to challenge and yet every one of the assumptions above will undermine it. Politicians are showing no sign of giving up those assumptions and are readily preventing and destroying the very thing they claim to want. This is not wilful, they simply do not understand the connection between the assumptions they espouse and the system they run.

'Is there a better set of assumptions? I hope Part One has shown that there is a very promising alternative. So far it is delivering better services at a much lower cost. We must continue to collect and share empirical evidence in order to prove its worth in the full range of circumstances that the citizenry can produce.

Conclusion

A call to arms

It's tempting to say what are you waiting for? There are many good people showing what can be done and there's nothing to lose. The worst that can happen is that you make a difference to some peoples' lives and save a lot of public money in the process.

Of course it's not quite that simple but neither is it difficult. In summary, we have found that we need to change the way we think. We have become inured to a corrosive normality. In striving to make public services accountable and good value for money we have made them unaccountable and shocking value for money. We didn't mean to, we just didn't know how to do it differently. Well now we do, so there is no excuse and no hiding place. Change will happen by getting knowledge. That knowledge is all around you. You barely have to look for it; you simply have to change the way you see it. I think this is a good definition of leadership – helping others learn to see.

Don't try and fix anything to start with, just go and learn. Take some typical citizens in your system who probably need help and learn what has happened to them over time. Build some case histories and see what is and is not typical of your system. Collect some data about those histories and find out how much it has cost to achieve what has been achieved, both positive and negative.

> **Health**: *take any typical person who attends their GP surgery or hospital with any regularity and look at what has been done over time and what difference it has made to their stability and independence.*

> **Police**: *talk to the neighbourhood teams and find out who the local people or families are that are known to everyone. Talk to the special needs coordinator at the local schools – they will tell you which families are struggling and which kids might be about to become the next generation of criminals. Collect information from all agencies and see what the history is and what it has or has not achieved.*

> **Housing**: *this is the easiest. Take some rent arrears cases and follow the people (not the rent arrears) over time and see what has caused what.*

> **Local authorities**: *use the range of indicators that the Stoke team used – it will be good enough to get you started. It should also be easy to work with your housing associations if you have no stock yourselves.*

Words of warning: I may have inspired you to get started by 'fixing' some people. Don't do this until you have some knowledge of them and the context of their lives. Take any chance you get to ask the key question of your citizens, 'What would a good life look like for you?' Experiment with different forms of the question to find something you are comfortable with and one that you find people respond to. Remember that your ears are the best bit of kit that you've got.

I'll finish with a low-key plug. The Vanguard website has plenty of useful information and guidance about how to go about things. The e–learning programmes on the site will give you plenty ideas and help.

Good luck.

About the Author

Richard Davis studied psychology at University College London before doing a masters at Lancaster in Behaviour in Organisations.

He then studied job information systems in the air transport industry and moved into training, becoming training manager for Avis, UK. While there he was leading the work to revive the exceptional service culture that had been developed under Colin Marshal (later of British Airways).

He came across the work of John Seddon showing how the system drives behaviour and the task began to make sense. Richard joined John at Vanguard UK in 1990 and has worked as a consultant ever since. He has worked in the private, public and voluntary sectors but of late has focused on the public sector and how to design services that help people and communities thrive rather than just fixing problems and needs.

About the Publisher

Triarchy Press is an independent publisher of alternative thinking (altThink) about government, organisations and society at large – as well as the people who participate in them.

Other titles by about the application of The Vanguard Method in practice include:

The Whitehall Effect - John Seddon

Systems Thinking in the Public Sector - John Seddon

Delivering Public Services that Work (Volume 1). Systems Thinking in the Public Sector Case Studies - Peter Middleton, John Seddon

Delivering Public Services that Work (Volume 2). The Vanguard Method in the Public Sector: Case Studies - Charlotte Pell, John Seddon

Other Triarchy Press titles on organisations, leadership, systems thinking and the public sector include:

Ackoff's F/Laws: The Cake - Russ Ackoff

Growing Wings on the Way: Systems Thinking for Messy Situations - Rosalind Armson

Humanising Healthcare - Margaret Hannah

Intelligent Policing - Simon Guilfoyle

Managers as Designers in the Public Services - David Wastell

Systems Thinking for Curious Managers - Russ Ackoff *et al.*

The Search for Leadership: An Organisational Perspective - William Tate

Details of all these titles and others are at:

www.triarchypress.net

Lightning Source UK Ltd.
Milton Keynes UK
UKOW06f0056141116
287493UK00006B/54/P